AF323193

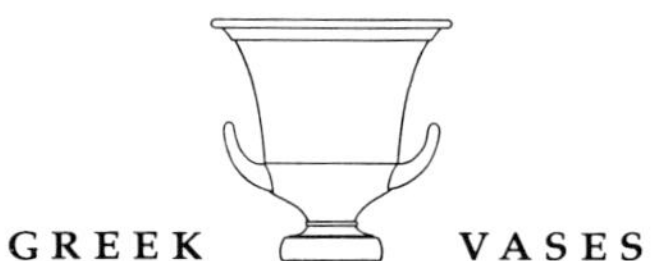

GREEK VASES

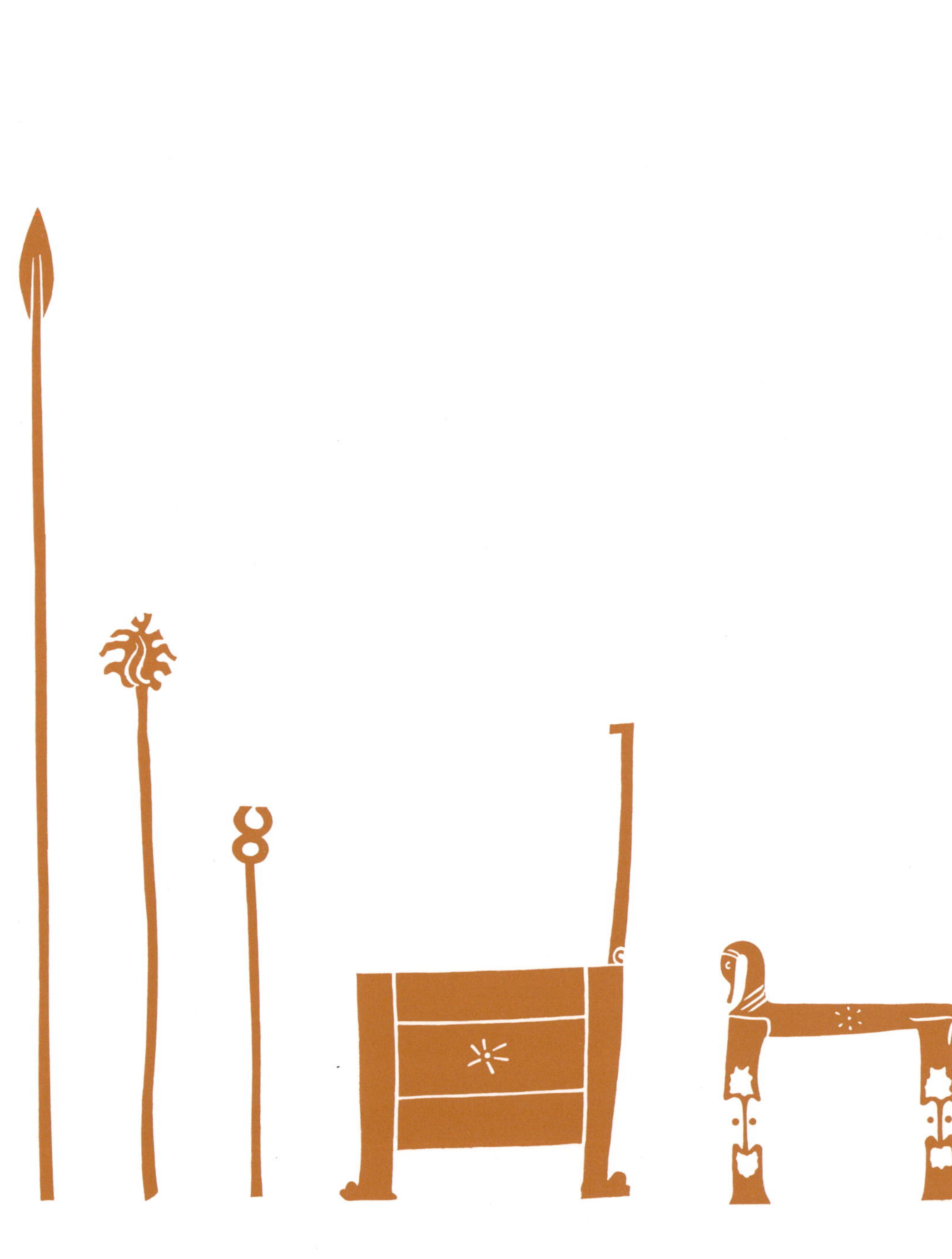

GREEK VASES

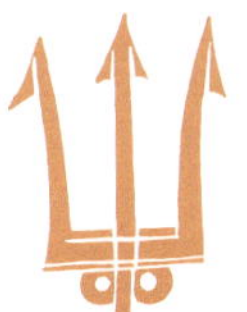

A GUIDE TO THE YALE COLLECTION
BY SUSAN B. MATHESON

YALE UNIVERSITY ART GALLERY

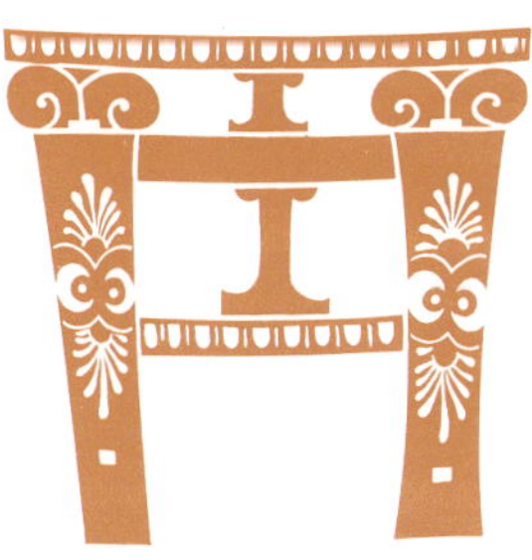

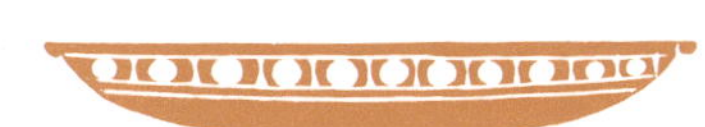

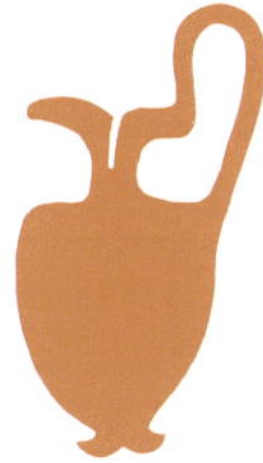

This project is supported by a grant
from the National Endowment for the Arts.

COVER:
Detail of Calyx Krater
by the Aegisthus Painter,
page 26 in this publication.

Copyright © 1988 by the Yale University Art Gallery.
All rights reserved.
Library of Congress Catalogue Number: 88–050027.
International Standard Book Number: 0–89467–048–4.
Manufactured in Japan.
Published by Yale University Art Gallery
2006 Yale Station, New Haven, Connecticut 06520.

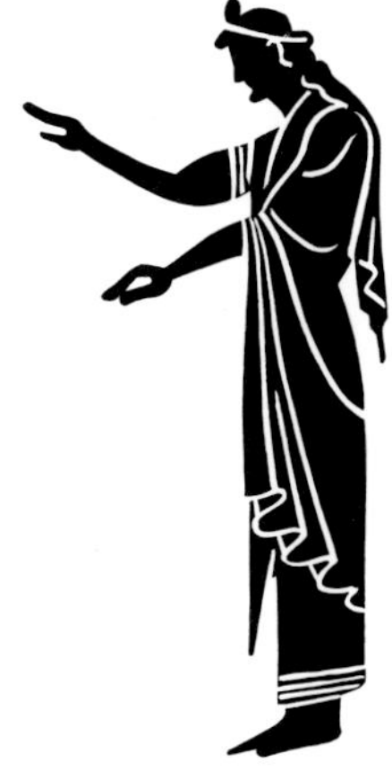

FOREWORD

In 1913 Mrs. Rebecca Darlington Stoddard of New Haven purchased for
Yale University the collection of Greek and Italian vases that bears her
name. Rebecca Darlington, originally from Pittsburgh, was educated at
Miss Porter's School in Farmington, Connecticut, and married Major
Louis E. Stoddard in 1904. Major Stoddard was a graduate of Yale (Class of
1899), and went on to be a noted polo player and President of the U.S. Polo
Association. The Stoddards set up housekeeping on Prospect Street in New
Haven. In 1913, Mrs. Stoddard approached Yale with an offer to buy
something for the University, and it was agreed that she would donate the
cost of a collection of ancient vases that was coming up for auction in Paris.
Yale's bid was successful and the collection was on its way to New Haven
when, on December 13th, Mrs. Stoddard died in childbirth. She never saw
the vases which were the foundation of Yale's holdings in Greek art.

The Stoddard collection, which numbered over nine hundred vases, was
actually one of several formed by Dr. Paul Arndt of Munich, a professor
and noted scholar in the field of Greek art in the late 19th and early 20th
centuries. The nucleus of the collection (some five hundred vases) was
bought in Paris in 1900 from the son and heir of an earlier collector and
supplemented with additional purchases for more than a decade. It appears
that Dr. Arndt selected this group of vases because they formed a sort of
visual encyclopaedia of ancient Mediterranean pottery from the Bronze
Age through the Roman Empire. Recent additions to the collection comple-
ment the Stoddard vases in key areas, but the great majority of the vases
the visitor sees at Yale are still those from the Stoddard gift.

Such a comprehensive and representative collection would, of course, be
particularly useful in teaching the history of Greek art, and it has served
that role at Yale. In addition, however, the Yale collection can provide to
everyone who sees it an introduction to most of the important aspects of
Greek pottery as well as to many interesting details of life in ancient
Greece. *Greek Vases: A Guide to the Yale Collection* is designed as an introduction to Greek vase painting from the Bronze Age through the fourth
century B.C., using as illustrations the vases in the Yale collection. The

Guide discusses the style, technique, and function of Greek vases, and also their subject matter, including myth, history, and scenes from daily life. It brings the viewer into contact with individual artists and gives a glimpse of the artistic, political, and commercial influences that created the environment in which they worked. The potters, the painters, and the Athenian and Italian patrons who bought their vases and buried them in their tombs have preserved for us a record of much of Greek life that is at once archaeologically instructive and artistically pleasing. This *Guide* is intended to add some basic information to the instinctive appreciation of the crisp forms, the glossy surfaces, and the elegant lines of ancient Greek vases.

It is a pleasure to acknowledge my debt to four colleagues whose thoughtful comments on the manuscript of this *Guide* did much to improve it: Professors Anne Coffin Hanson, Sarah P. Morris, and J. J. Pollitt, and Dr. Marion True. My sincere thanks also go to Sue Allen, whose elegant design has brought the book to life.

Susan B. Matheson

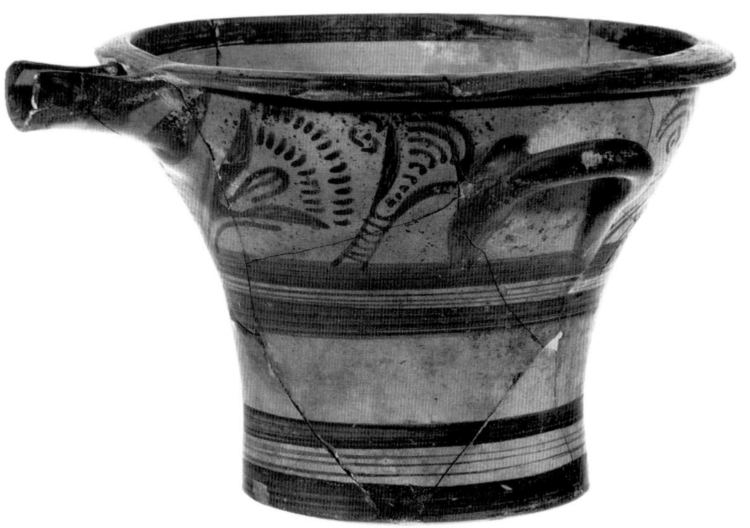

BRIDGE-SPOUTED BOWL

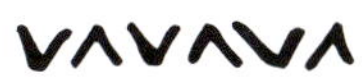

The final phase of the Greek Bronze Age, known as the Mycenaean period (ca. 1400-1125 B.C.), marked the emergence of mainland Greece as a commercial and military power in the Mediterranean, free from the competition of the older and more brilliant civilization of Minoan Crete. The palaces and citadels of Mycenae, Tiryns, and Pylos, among others, formed the bases of a well-organized, bureaucratic economic system that sponsored trade throughout the Mediterranean world.

The pottery produced in the Mycenaean period provides some of the best evidence for the extent of this trade. The characteristic stirrup jar, for example, was filled with perfumed oil and exported eastward to Asia Minor, Cyprus, and the Syro-Palestinian coast as well as westward to Italy and Sicily.

Mycenaean pottery reflects the stylistic influences of Minoan Crete, whose artistic tradition dominated the Mediterranean in the earlier phases of the Middle and Late Bronze Age. Vessel shapes like the stirrup jar, the piriform jar, and the bridge-spouted bowl are derived from Minoan prototypes, and the decorative motifs on this pottery are shorthand formulaic versions of the exuberant naturalistic plant and marine motifs favored by Minoan vase painters. The repetitive nature of both vase forms and decorative motifs, however, is probably symptomatic of the mass production required by an extensive export industry.

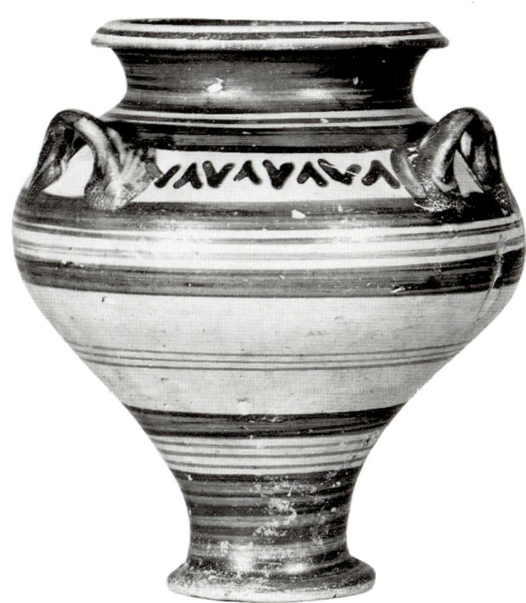

PIRIFORM JAR

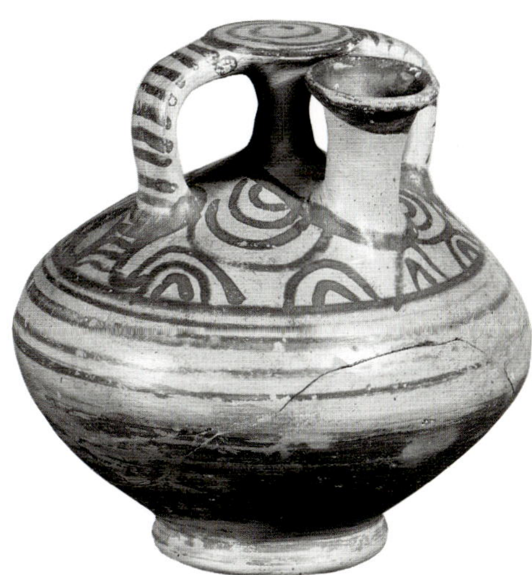

STIRRUP JAR

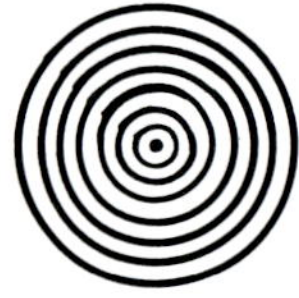

Little is known about the two centuries following the fall of Mycenaean civilization in Greece, a period which is thus frequently referred to as the Dark Ages (ca. 1100-900 B.C.). With no written records for this period, archaeological evidence provides the only basis for interpretation of its history. Most of the remains come from cemeteries, and they suggest significant changes in customs. A new style of long bronze pin found in these tombs, for example, suggests a new style of dress. A few of these pins are made of iron, a material not generally used before this date. The style of the tombs themselves underwent a major change, and cremation burial was introduced, with pottery vessels such as this amphora serving as ash urns.

These cultural changes were matched, in the pottery, by changes in style. The echoes of Minoan naturalism seen in Mycenaean pottery gave way to the earliest manifestations of the Geometric style that dominated Greek art in the succeeding two centuries (ca. 900-700 B.C.). The concentric circles on the shoulder of this amphora are characteristic Protogeometric motifs that continue in Geometric art. A compass with a multiple brush was a contemporary technical innovation that enabled the vase painter to draw the motif with precision.

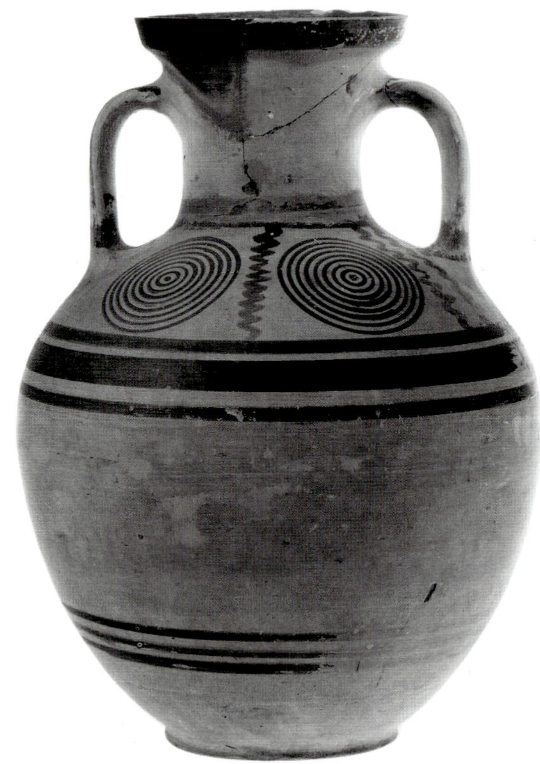

PROTOGEOMETRIC AMPHORA

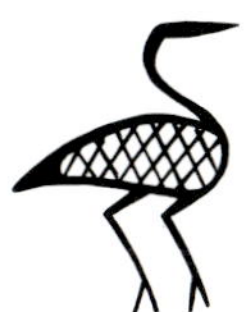

A proliferation of geometric ornament organized in a complex system of banded decoration characterizes the pottery of the Late Geometric period. A large repertoire of geometric motifs (e.g. triangles, meanders, lozenges, checkerboards, zigzags, chevrons, etc.) was manipulated by the vase painter into a system of bands and panels that simultaneously covers the surface of the vase and emphasizes its major architectonic parts. A similar process of creating large works of art from varied combinations of repeated formulae is the basis for the first great poetic works in Greece, the *Iliad* and *Odyssey* of Homer, which were composed during the Geometric period.

Birds, animals, and occasionally human forms were introduced into the system, but they, too, were "geometricized." The Geometric artist tended to analyze his figures, like the vases themselves, into their component parts, emphasizing the most important of them in his stylized representations. The long legs and arching neck of a horse, the long sinuous neck and spindly legs of a water bird, and the small head, triangular upper body, and tiny waist of a man represent the artist's understanding of the essential nature of these figures.

The flowering of the Geometric style took place particularly in Athens, but there were local variations of the style as well in other areas of mainland Greece and the Greek Islands. These local styles are symptomatic of important historical developments during this period, especially the growth of the city states, which were to be the dominant political unit in later Greek history, and an increase in population that encouraged overseas colonization and trade.

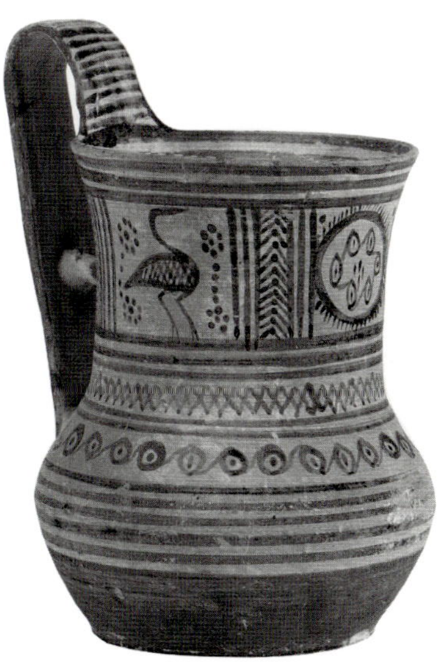

OLPE

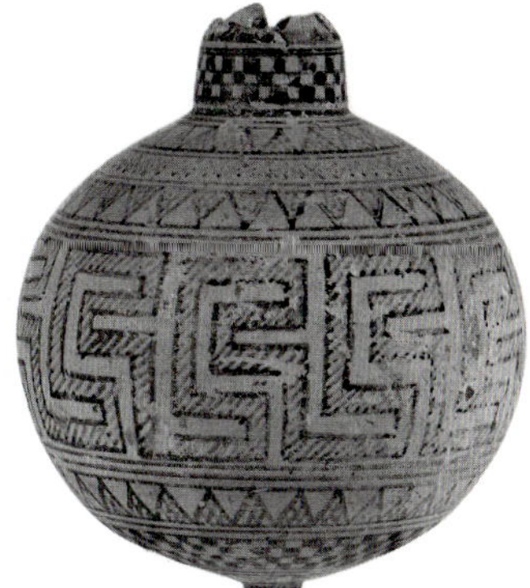

POMEGRANATE VASE

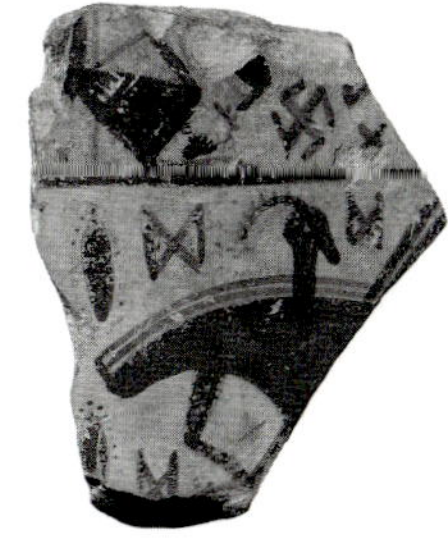

FRAGMENT
WITH WARRIORS

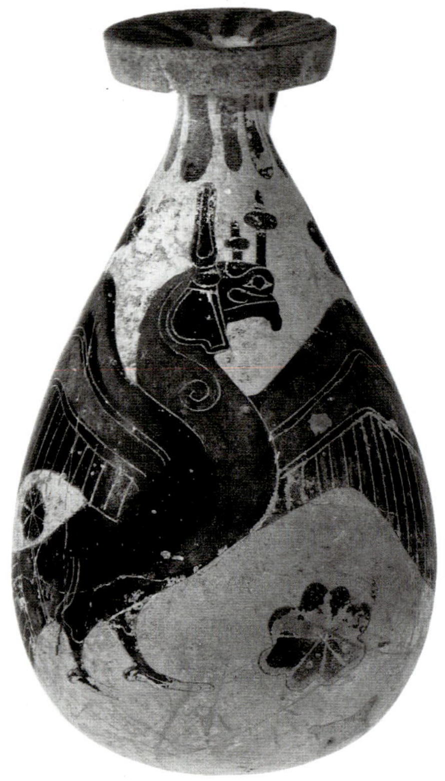

Corinthian Griffin-bird Alabastron

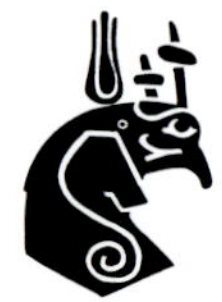

The Orientalizing period, which succeeded the Geometric period during the eighth century B.C., owes its modern name to the growing influence of Near Eastern cultures on Greece brought about by trade at this time. Foremost among the Greek traders were the merchants of Corinth, a city whose geographic position gave it control over the only transfer point between the western sea trade routes to Italy and Sicily and the eastern routes through the Aegean Sea to Cyprus and the eastern Mediterranean.

Into Corinthian ports came metalwork, ivories, and probably textiles and other perishable goods in the heraldic style of Syrian, Assyrian, and Neo-Hittite art, with subjects drawn from a repertoire of fantastic hybrid mythical beasts characteristic of Near Eastern art. Sphinxes, gorgons, sirens, griffins, centaurs, and similar creatures were adopted by Corinthian artists, whose pottery, in particular, features combinations of real and mythical beasts in a style almost completely devoted to animals.

Small pottery vessels filled with perfumed oil were Corinth's major export, and containers like this alabastron with a "griffin-bird" (the eagle-headed griffin normally had a lion's body) have been found in large num-

10

bers throughout the Mediterranean. Up until the early sixth century B.C., the Corinthian animal style influenced contemporary vase painters in Athens, where the so-called Proto-Attic and early Attic styles relied heavily on Corinthian animal frieze and heraldic groupings. Corinthian vase painters are credited with an important technical innovation as well, the black-figure technique, which Athenian vase painters adopted and made famous.

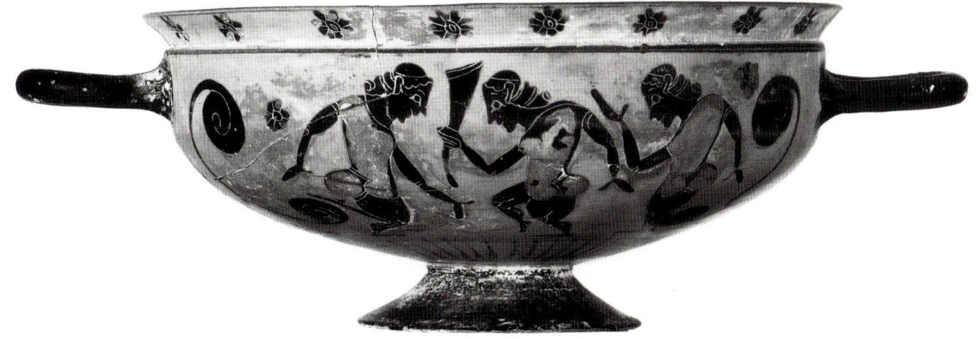

KOMAST CUP

Early Attic Black-figure Komast Cup by the KY Painter

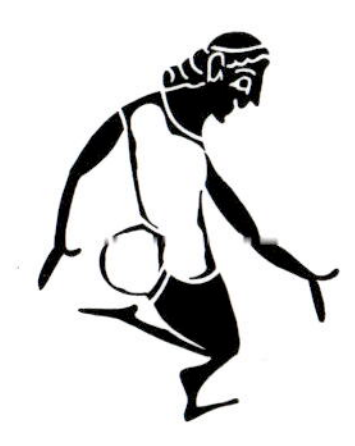

Early Attic (Athenian) vase painting is directly derived from the black-figure animal style vases of Corinth. The black-figure technique, in which the painted silhouette that forms the figure is incised before firing to indicate interior details, flowered during the sixth century B.C. into one of the major art forms of Archaic Athens.

Predictably, the earliest Athenian black-figure vases are closest to their Corinthian prototypes. This cup by an Athenian artist called the KY Painter is largely an imitation of a Corinthian version, echoing the prototype in shape, ornament, and subject. The three dancing figures on each side, called *komast* dancers (from the Greek word *komos*, "revel"), are related to satyrs and Dionysos. They have the stocky proportions of their Corinthian counterparts, and one carries a *rhyton* (a drinking vessel) like those seen on Corinthian cups. The komast dancers wear padding on their buttocks, a detail which may link them to the origins of Greek drama, since they seem to have been associated with the dancers and mimes that were antecedents of both tragedy and comedy. Padded costumes survived in Attic comedy down to the fourth century B.C.

11

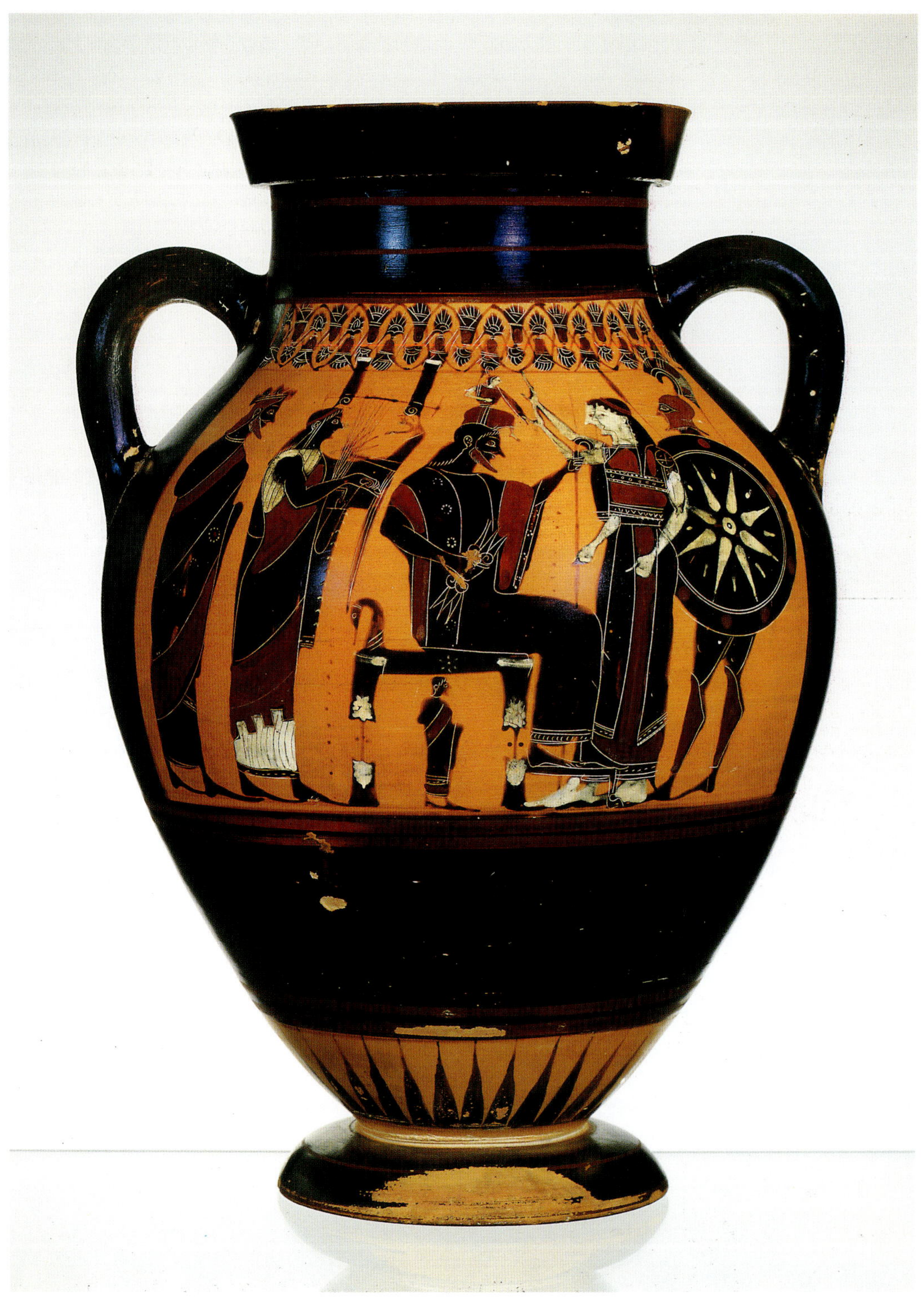

By the middle of the sixth century B.C., the pottery workshops in the
Kerameikos (the potters' quarter) in Athens were well established and pro-
ducing black-figure vases of excellent quality for local use and for export to
the flourishing Greek colonies in Italy. Among the most prolific of these
was a workshop conventionally called Group E, which was active between
around 560 and 540 B.C. The painters of this group show strong familial
similarities to one another, both in details of drawing (i.e., incision) and in
choice of subject. Group E has been considered by some scholars to be the
environment from which Exekias, the greatest of all black-figure vase
painters, developed.

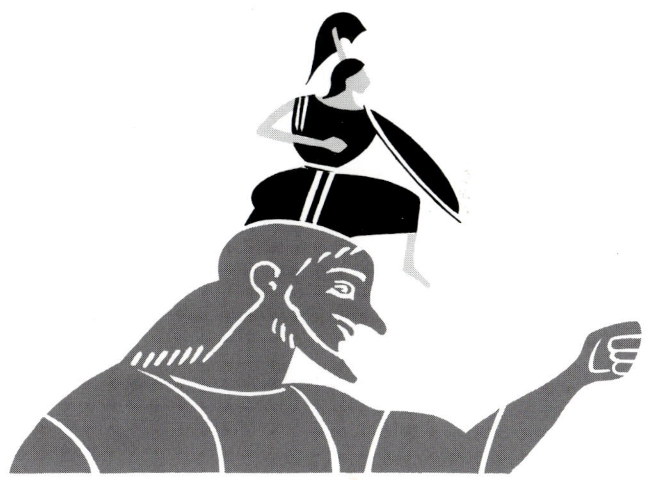

ATHENA EMERGING FROM ZEUS' HEAD

This amphora (storage jar) by an artist in Group E shows two subjects
which were favored by the Group. On one side the goddess Athena is born,
fully clothed and armed, from the head of her father, Zeus, as described by
Hesiod in the *Theogony*. The birth of Athena is attended by other gods,
from left to right, Dionysos, Apollo, the Eileithyiae (twin goddesses of
childbirth), and Ares. A four-horse chariot, seen from the front, appears on
the second side of the vase. The charioteer's long white garment (a *chiton*)
and the added red details of the horses' manes add extra vibrancy to the essentially two-color black-figure scheme.

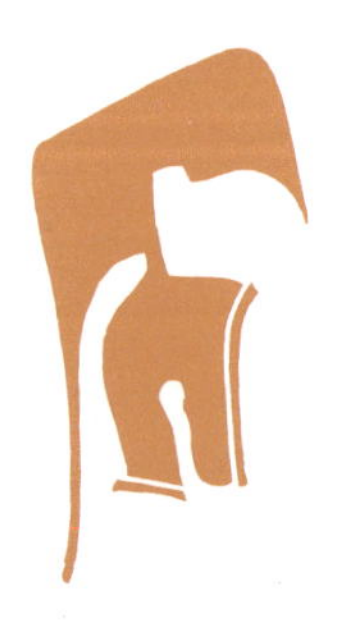

Around 530 B.C. Athenian vase painters discovered that the black-figure technique could be essentially reversed to create a method of decoration now known as red-figure. Whereas in black-figure vases the figures were drawn as black silhouettes against a background of unpainted (reserved) clay, the red-figure artist left the figures reserved, surrounding their natural clay surface with a background of lustrous black glaze. Interior details of anatomy and decoration, which had been incised in the black-figure silhouettes, were now drawn with a brush in a thick solution of black glaze on the reserved clay figures.

The red-figure technique tends to focus the viewer's eye on the individual figures to a greater extent than does black-figure. The black background seems to make the figures stand out in three dimensions, and the use of a brush results in a fluid line that allows for greater articulation of the figure's interior structure. Greek vase-painters exploited this quality in a variety of innovative and experimental ways during the decades following the introduction of the new technique. By the second quarter of the fifth century B.C., the more versatile red-figure technique had essentially replaced black-figure for all but the prize vases from the Panathenaic games (see p. 20).

The invention of the red-figure technique took place during the years in which Athens was ruled by the tyrant Peisistratos and his sons (560-510 B.C.). Important developments in Greek literary history also took place in the Peisistratid era. Among these were the first written compilations of epic poems like the *Iliad* and *Odyssey* of Homer, and the introduction into the Panathenaic games of a contest for the recitation of these epics, both probably at the instigation of Peisistratos himself. As might be expected, such official sponsorship of epic poetry led to the increasingly widespread appearance of epic subjects in art, subjects such as that shown on this early red-figure plate by the vase painter Paseas.

The abduction of the Trojan prophetess Kassandra shown here is drawn from the story of the sack of Troy, described in at least two lost Greek epic poems. Kassandra is shown nude, clutching the drapery of the statue of Athena, to which she has fled for safety and from which her abductor, Ajax, the son of Oileus, is dragging her away. Kassandra's gaze is fixed on Athena, but the painter, Paseas, has drawn the viewer's eye to the center of the composition, to the point where Ajax's hand grasps Kassandra's arm, which is in turn linked over the arm of the Athena statue, the refuge that failed. This overlapping conjunction could not have been represented successfully in black-figure, suggesting that Paseas has understood and consciously exploited the potential of the new red-figure technique to emphasize the dramatic and religious conflicts in the scene.

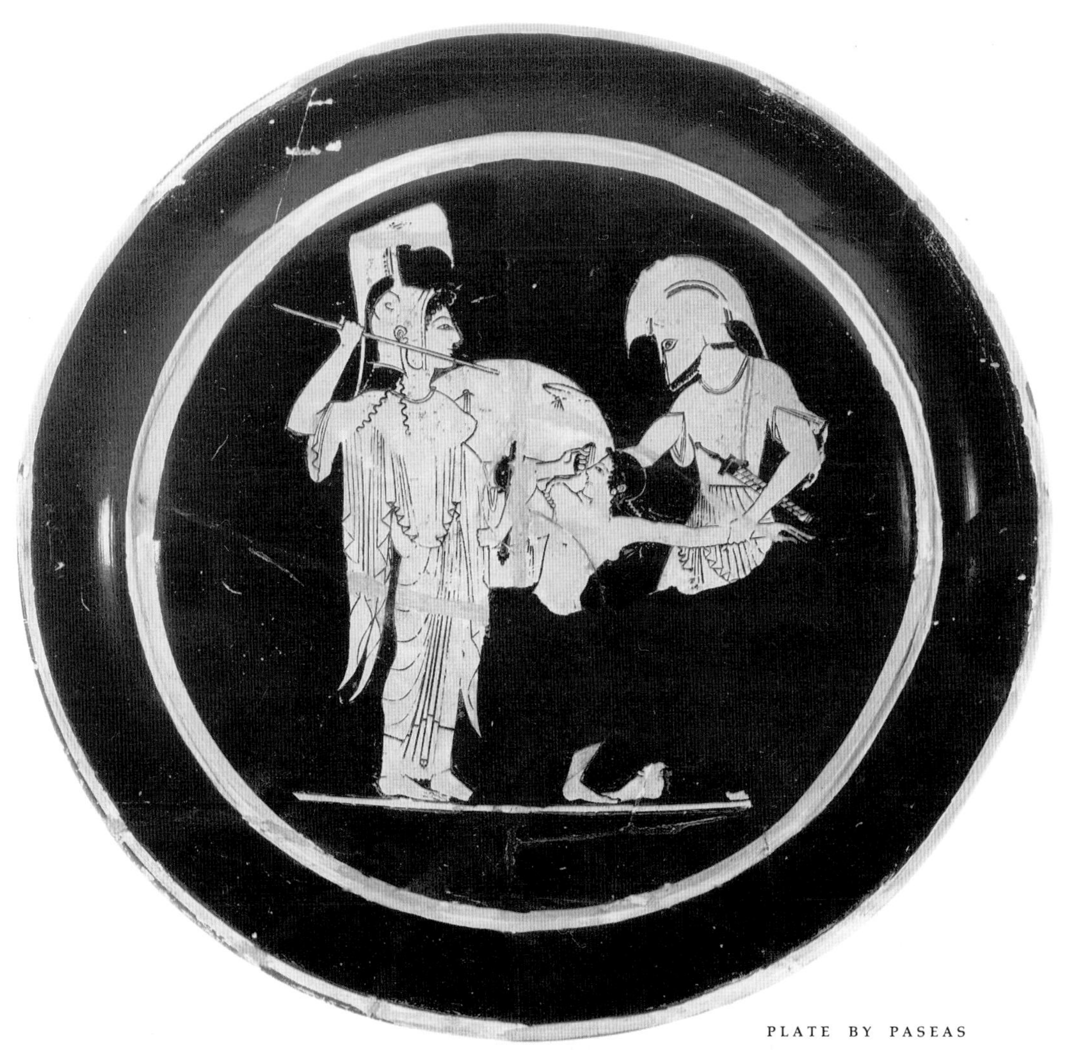

PLATE BY PASEAS

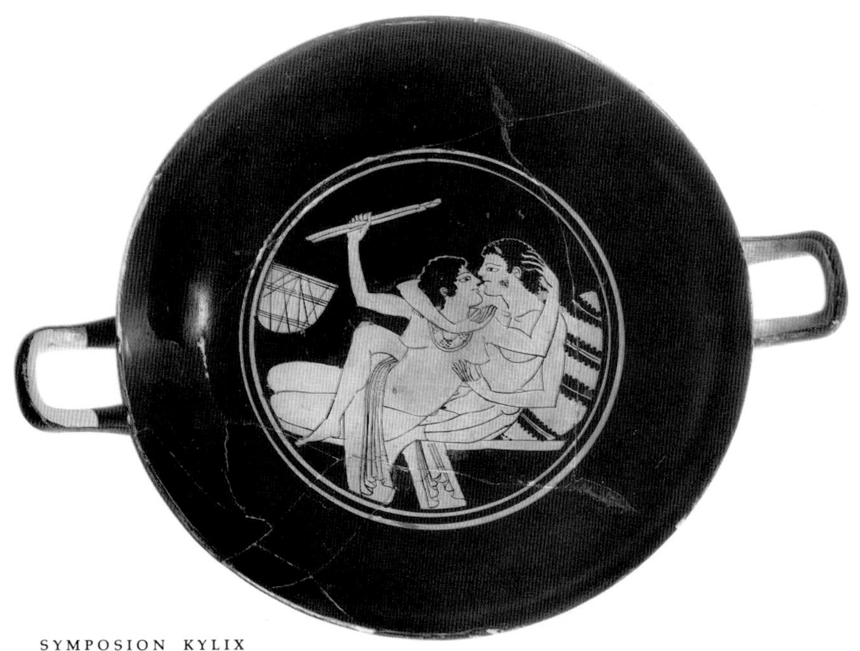

SYMPOSION KYLIX

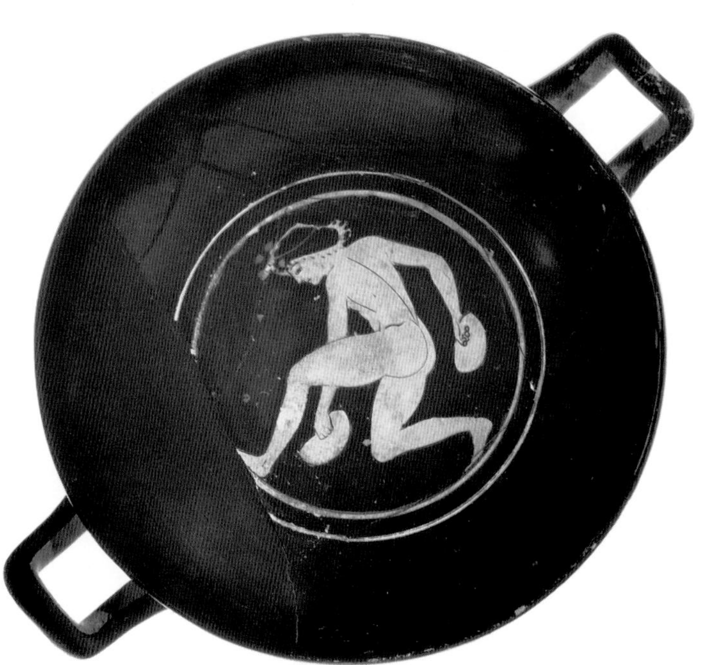

KYLIX WITH JUMPER

16

Early experimenters in the red-figure technique, painters like Euphronios, Euthymides, and the so-called Pioneers, explored ways of representing the human body as it moved, twisted, and turned in space, and as it related to other figures moving in the same space. Artists experimented widely with back views and foreshortened figures. Wrestling, running, jumping (left, below), and other athletic activities became popular vehicles for these figural studies. The interaction of men and women (prostitutes or professional entertainers) at drinking parties provided further opportunities for the portrayal of overlapping and partly foreshortened figures (left, above). Both types of activities would have been familiar to the aristocratic Athenians who owned and used these drinking cups and other vessels at parties (*symposia*) such as that represented here.

The artists who painted these two cups have treated the circular format quite differently. The drinking party, with its young man and his paid companion reclining on a couch that extends beyond the circular frame, is seen as if through a round window. The jumper, on the other hand, is balanced on the circular frame itself, which serves as a groundline for the figure's twisting movement. The objects the jumper holds are weights (*halteres*), used in the long jump to increase distance.

When viewed obliquely, the symposion cup shows the preliminary sketch drawn by the artist with a sharp instrument before applying the black glaze. In the finished drawing, he has changed the position of the young man's knee to increase the sense of foreshortening.

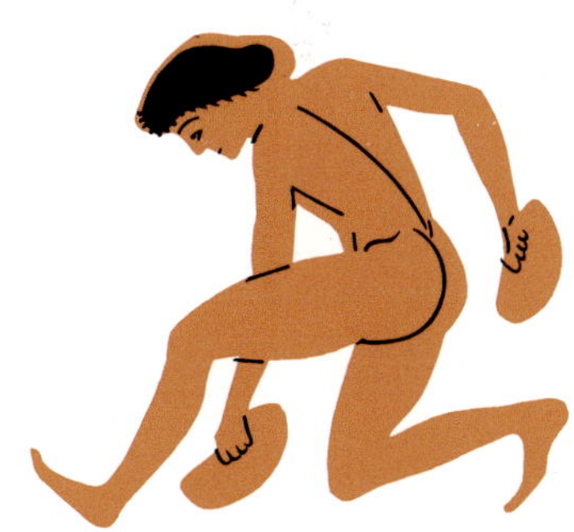

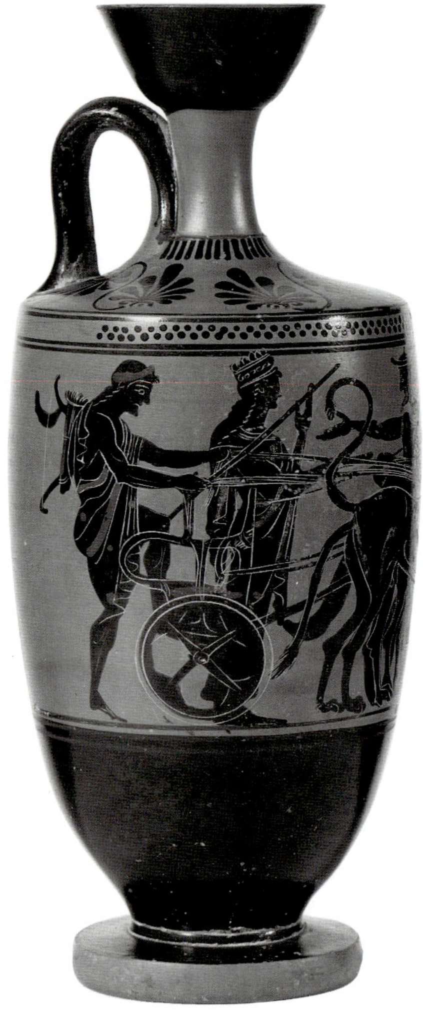

LEKYTHOS WITH DIVINE CHARIOT

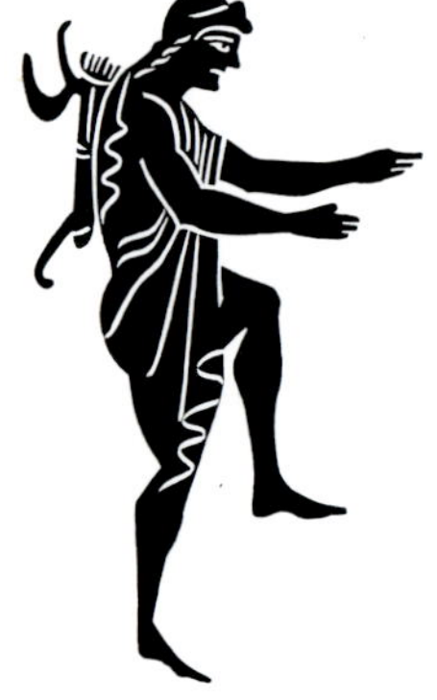

Artists continued to paint vases in the black-figure technique for at least fifty years after the invention of red-figure. Quite a few artists painted vases in both techniques, or artistic languages, with a few of the earliest red-figure painters combining the two techniques on a single vase (called a "bilingual" vase). The majority of the black-figure vases painted in the "red-figure period" were close cousins to their contemporary red-figure counterparts in shape, ornament, and style. Occasionally attempts at foreshortening and other experimental features were tried, but as they met with predictably less success in the old silhouette technique, black-figure

18

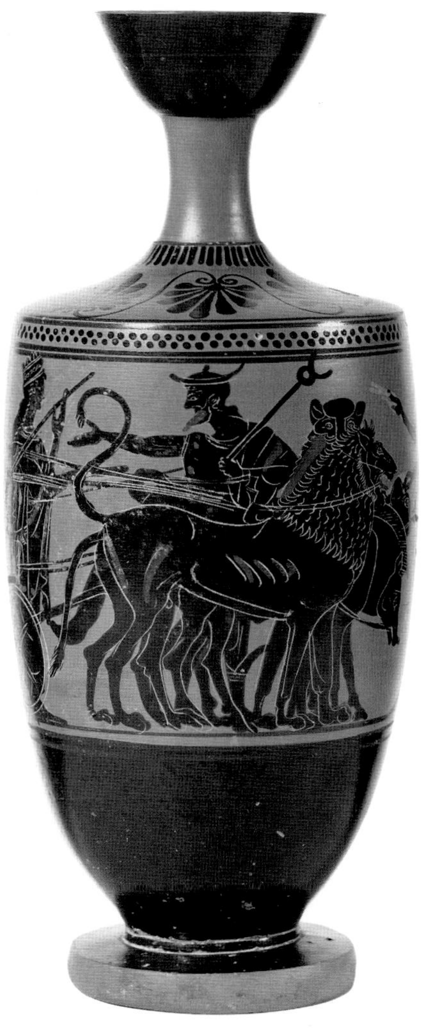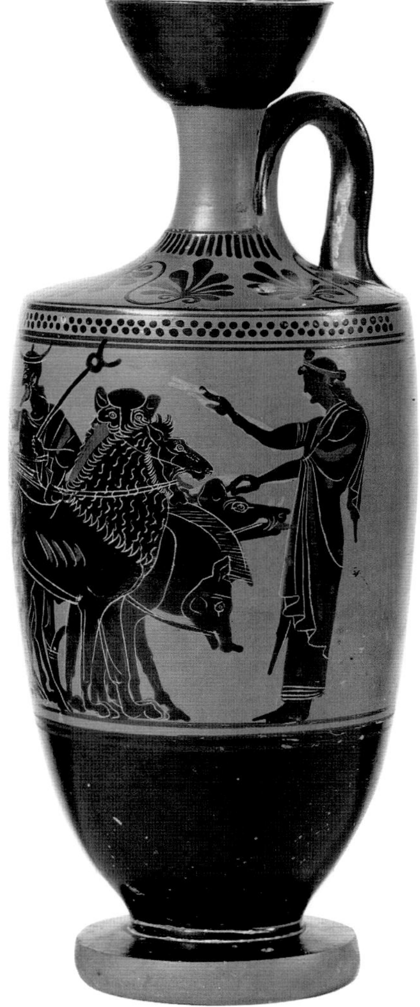

painters tended to stick to more staid, frieze-like subjects such as chariot scenes, processions, and single combats.

This *lekythos* (oil container) by the Edinburgh Painter shows a standard, but finely drawn, scene of a chariot driven by Apollo, who is accompanied by his mother Leto (next to him), his sister Artemis (far right), and Hermes, the god of journeys. Less standard is the combination of animals that pull the chariot: a pair of boars joined to a pair of lions, an unlikely team for any driver but a god.

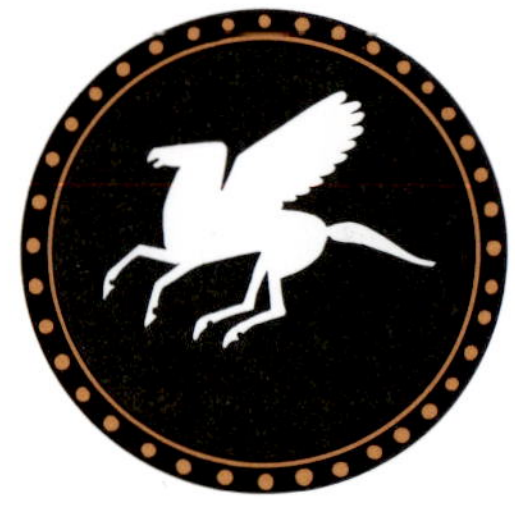

The prizes in the Panathenaic Games, held in Athens every four years to celebrate the birthday of the city's patron goddess, Athena, were a special type of vase filled with olive oil. The oil itself was the prize, but, after their introduction as part of the reorganization of the Panathenaic festival around 566 B.C., the containers in which the oil was presented came to symbolize victory in these important games. The prize vases, a special type of amphora, were commissioned by the Athenian government, and the commissions generally seem to have been given to the best workshops in the Kerameikos. This example is by the Kleophrades Painter, who is well known for his fine red-figure vases, and whose Panathenaic amphorae are among the few vases he painted in the black-figure technique. This vase is one of a pair of Panathenaics by this artist at Yale.

Panathenaic amphorae were essentially standardized in shape and decoration by around 530 B.C., and they retained their standard form as long as they were awarded as prizes, that is, as late as the Hellenistic period. The prize vases were always painted in the black-figure technique, which meant that this technique survived into the second century B.C., long after the production of other black-figure and red-figure vases had ceased. In the characteristic two-panel format, a striding figure of Athena, holding a shield and a raised spear, appears on the front between two columns topped by cocks. A standard inscription at the left states that the vase was "from the games at Athens." The back of the vase shows the contest for which it was a prize, in this case the four-horse chariot race, a major event. As in modern horse racing, the prize was awarded to the owner of the horses rather than to the driver, even though here it is the driver who is shown on the vase. Other Panathenaic amphorae depict foot races, relays, wrestling, boxing, a *pentathlon* (foot race, broad jump, wrestling, discus- and spear-throwing), and a foot race in armor, as well as poetry recitations and musical competitions.

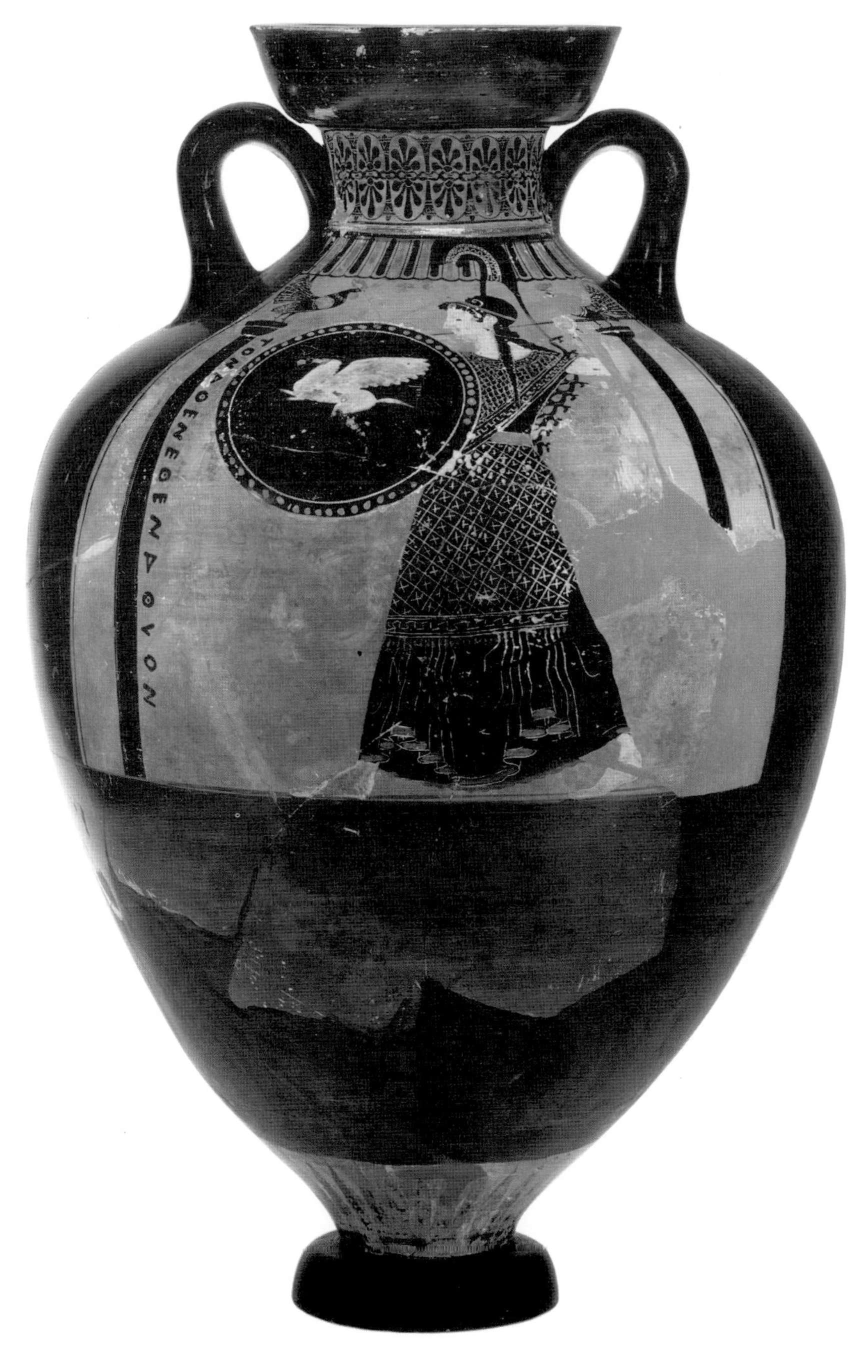

PANATHENAIC PRIZE VASE

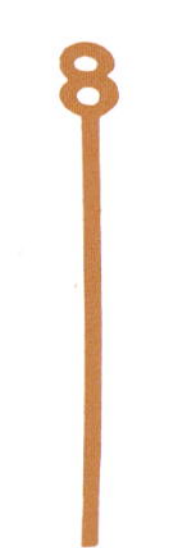

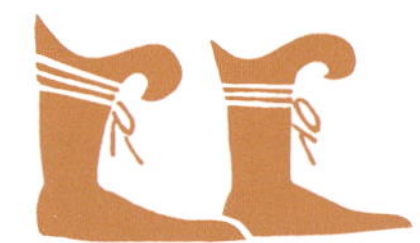

Late Archaic red-figure vase painting, i.e., red-figure vase painting from the late sixth and early fifth centuries B.C., is considered by many to be the high point of Greek vase painting. The nearly perfect balance between form and decoration achieved in the best Late Archaic vases results in works of art that can be appreciated simultaneously as refined drawings and as elegantly decorated vessels. Among the artists who created these elegant vases, the Berlin Painter is one of the acknowledged masters.

The Berlin Painter, like the Kleophrades Painter (see p. 20), belonged to the second generation of red-figure painters. By the early fifth century B.C., when both of these artists were active, the information gained from the experiments in foreshortening and other figural studies by the early Pioneers (see p. 17) had largely been assimilated, and the new generation preferred either to explore the potential for emotional expression through dramatic narrative, or, like the Berlin Painter in his innovative single-figure compositions, to concentrate on the purely aesthetic effect of ochre-colored figures against a black glaze.

By limiting himself to one figure on each side of the vase, here the Olympian gods Athena and Hermes, the Berlin Painter focuses the viewer's attention on the perfection of that one figure. The refined and delicate drawing and the careful attention to patterns of dress and other details can thus be seen to best advantage. The Berlin Painter keeps ornament to a minimum on his vases, avoiding competition with the figures. Here a short band of simple key pattern forms a platform for each figure to stand on. The single figures also harmonize naturally with the shape of the vase, echoing its vertical form, and each figure's outstretched arm emphasizes the vase's widest point.

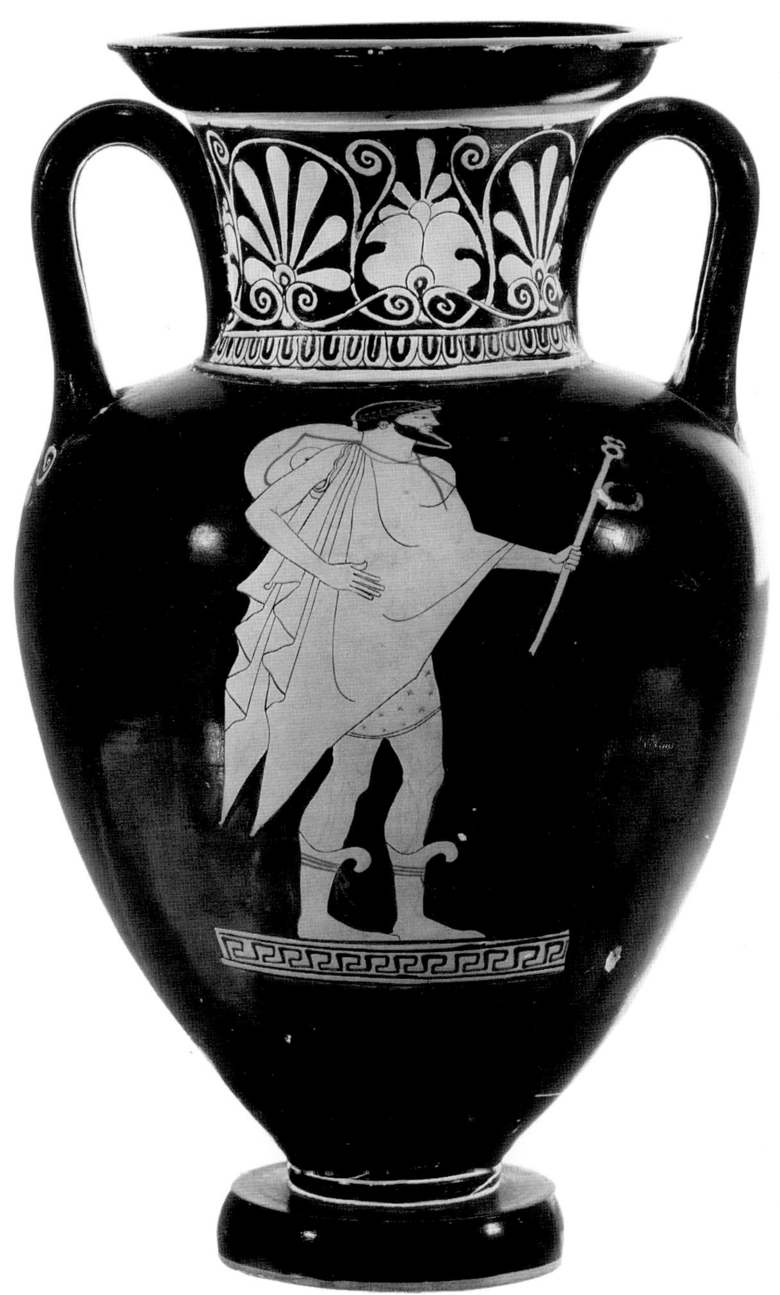

AMPHORA BY THE BERLIN PAINTER

Red-figure Kylix by the Brygos Painter

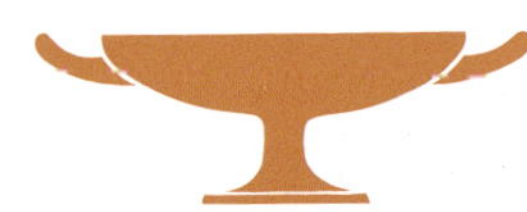

Painted vases were luxury items frequently used in the drinking parties (*symposia*) that formed such an important part of aristocratic Athenian life. Drinking cups (*kylikes* and *skyphoi*), along with mixing bowls and wine coolers (*kraters* and *psykters*), wine jars (*amphorae*), water jars (*hydrai*), pitchers (*oinochoai*), and ladles (*kyathoi*), were essential equipment for these affairs. The kylix appears to have been the most popular form of drinking cup, probably because it was especially well suited to the Greek custom of eating and drinking while reclining on a couch. Its decoration gave pleasure to both the drinker, who was "surprised" by the appearance of the design in the center of the cup as he finished his wine, and his companions, who could admire the decoration on the outside of the cup while he drank.

Scenes of drinking parties and the processions of revellers that followed them, and the satyr- and maenad-filled mythical equivalents of these real-life festivities, were favorite subjects for vessels associated with symposia, and particularly for cups. The Brygos Painter's versions of these scenes are especially lively, with exuberant participants who are obviously enjoying themselves.

The Brygos Painter was primarily a cup painter, and the symposion was one of his favorite subjects. The flute player on this cup may be part of a post-party procession, although the flaming altar before him may suggest instead a religious or sacrificial association. In any case, this musician shows intense involvement in his music as he leans back, puffs out his cheeks, and separates his double flutes to hit a high note. The Brygos Painter has skillfully adapted his composition to the circular format of the cup's interior, using the edge of the circle to make the figure's walking pose seem relaxed and natural.

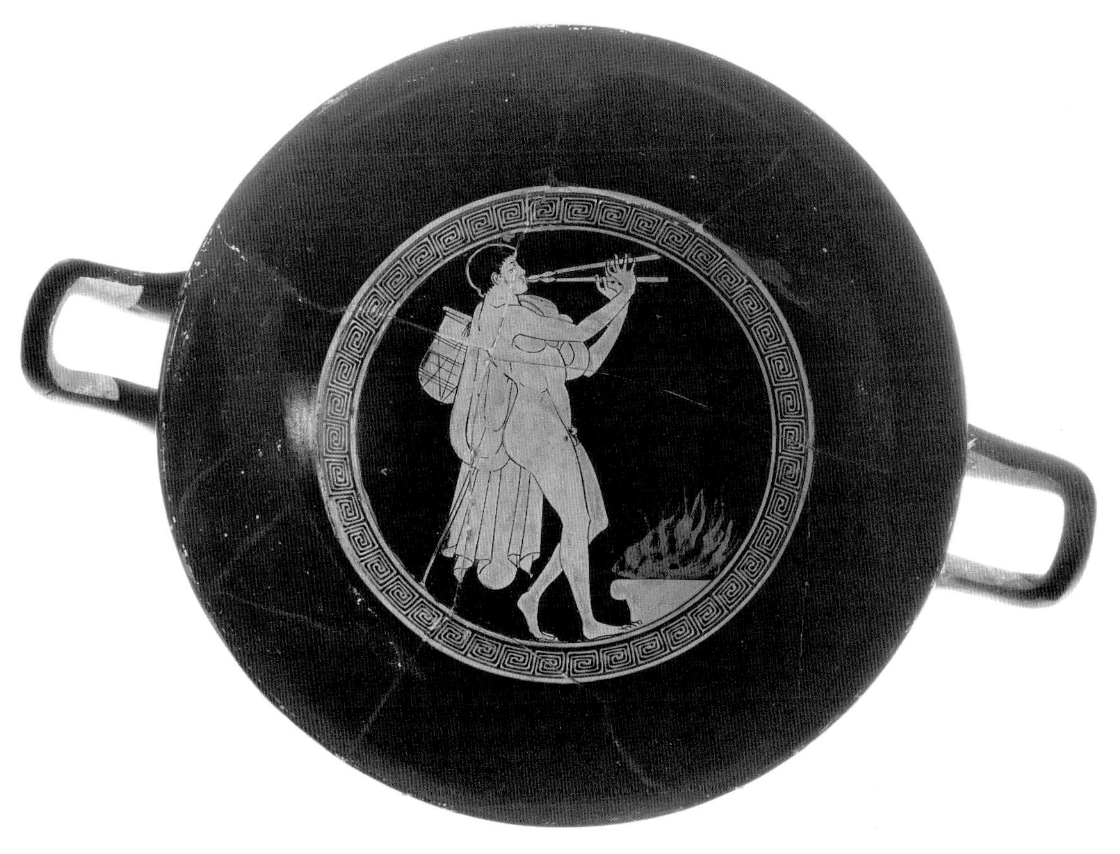

KYLIX BY THE BRYGOS PAINTER

The transition in Athenian vase painting from the Late Archaic to the Early Classical style around the 470s B.C. is paralleled over a somewhat longer period by a similar and related change in Greek sculpture. In sculpture, the Early Classical style reached its high point in the famous pediments and metopes of the Temple of Zeus at Olympia (462-457 B.C.). The change can be described in part as one from a rather angular style with an intense love of pattern and ornament to a more ''severe'' style, with large solid forms and rounder, more naturalistic, and ultimately more fluid drapery. Early Classical figures are noble and stately, even in action, and for the first time their character, their emotions, and their psychological interactions are shown.

The beginnings of the Early Classical style can be seen in this impressive red-figure calyx krater by the Aegisthus Painter, dating to around 475-470 B.C. The vase represents Nike, the winged goddess of victory, pouring an offering of wine to the enthroned sea god Poseidon, who holds his trident and a *phiale* (an offering dish) in which to receive the wine. The large simple forms used for the sleeves and skirts of the garments (*chitons*) worn by both figures are characteristic of the solid ''severe'' forms of Early Classical vase painting and sculpture. Nike's large round chin and the straight line of the profile of her forehead and nose (suggesting the profile of a Corinthian helmet) are also hallmarks of the Early Classical style. The figures lean back slightly, echoing the profile of the vase, a feature which combines with a still rather liberal use of ornamental detail to recall the vase's Late Archaic predecessors. The Aegisthus Painter provides the transition from the Late Archaic Berlin Painter (see p. 22) to the Early Classical Painter of the Yale Oinochoe (see p. 28).

The pairing on the Aegisthus Painter's krater of the goddess of victory and the god of the sea may refer to important events in Athenian history, as does the combination of Theseus and Poseidon on the Yale Oinochoe painted a few years later. On the krater, Nike (Victory) offers thanks to the power of the sea, who personifies in turn the power of the Athenian navy, the key to the Athenian victory in the Persian wars.

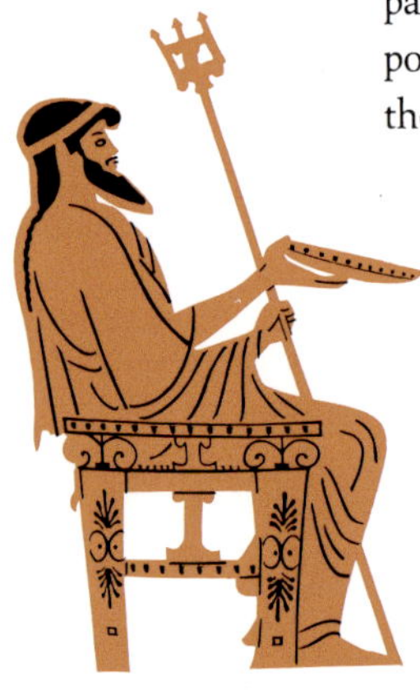

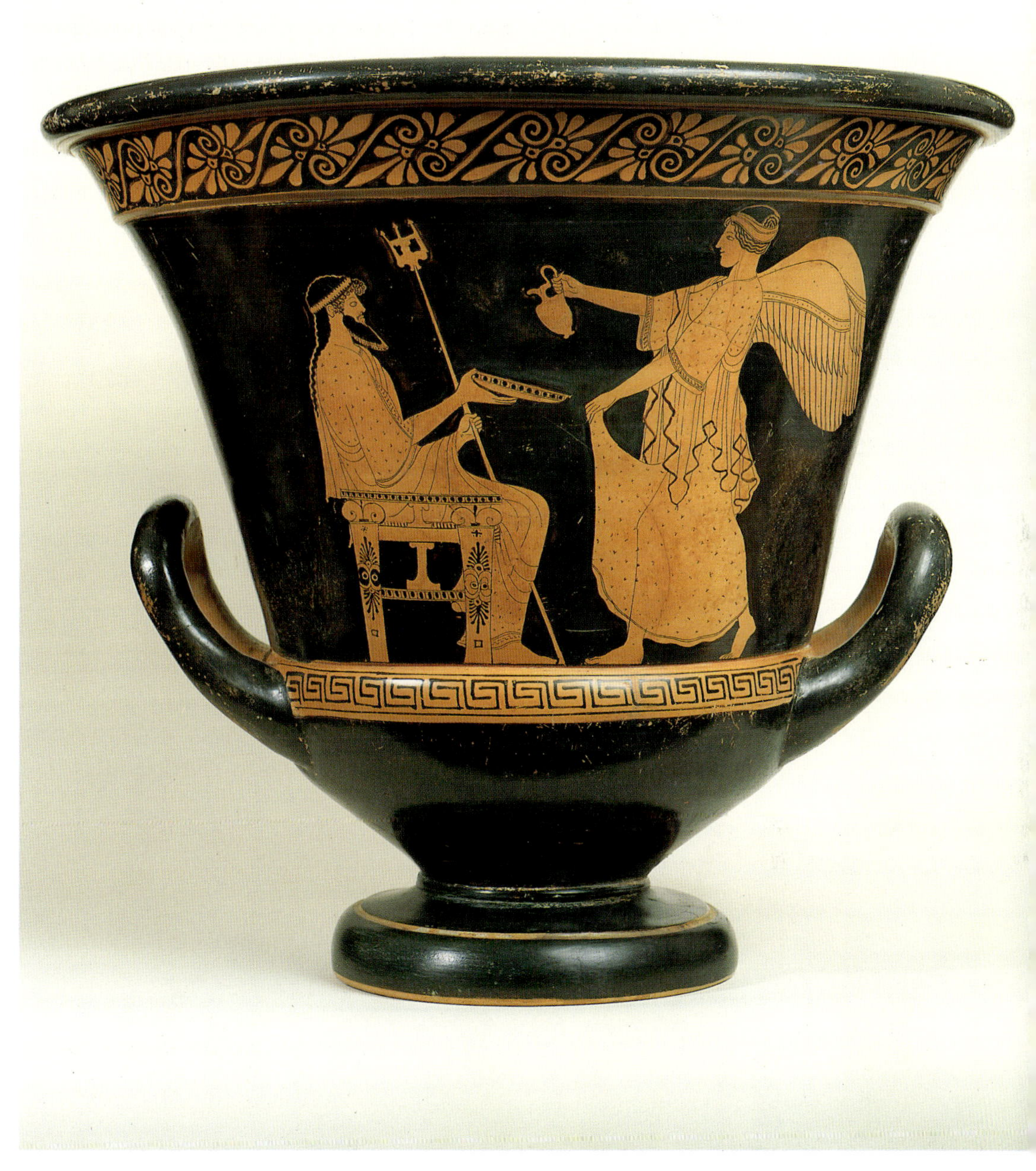

CALYX KRATER SHOWING NIKE AND POSEIDON

This unusually large *oinochoe* (pitcher) is the so-called "name vase" of the Painter of the Yale Oinochoe. Relatively few Greek vase painters signed their works, and so the vast majority of vases are by painters whose real names are unknown to us today. By isolating similarities of stylistic details in the vases, scholars have collected groups of vases which can be attributed to individual artists, and have created names (or nicknames) for these artists. The names are generally based on the location of one of the artist's vases (e.g., the Berlin Painter, the Painter of the Yale Oinochoe), the name of a known potter for whom the painter worked (e.g., the Brygos Painter, the Kleophrades Painter), or an especially notable characteristic of the artist's style (e.g., a painter called "Elbows Out").

The Painter of the Yale Oinochoe is a fully developed Early Classical artist, as the rather simplified forms and fluid drapery lines of this vase attest. Equally characteristic of the Early Classical style is the exchange of glances between the two figures, Poseidon and Theseus.

Poseidon (left), holding his trident, acknowledges his son, Theseus, with a handshake. Theseus was the national hero of Athens, who was believed, among other helpful feats, to have appeared at the battle of Marathon in 490 B.C. to aid the Athenians in their fight against the Persians. In 475 B.C., shortly before this vase was made, bones said to be those of Theseus were brought to Athens and a cult was established there in his honor. Representations of Theseus on vases increased at this time, reflecting, perhaps, patriotic feelings associated with the Athenian victory in the Persian Wars. Poseidon, the sea god, was also thought to have played an important role in the Athenian victory, in that he, along with Boreas, the god of the north wind, was held responsible for a storm that destroyed a large portion of the Persian fleet in the straits off Salamis in 480 B.C. Together the two figures can be viewed as symbols of a prosperous and powerful post-war Athens (Theseus) acknowledging the powers that support it, the Athenian fleet and the sea (Poseidon).

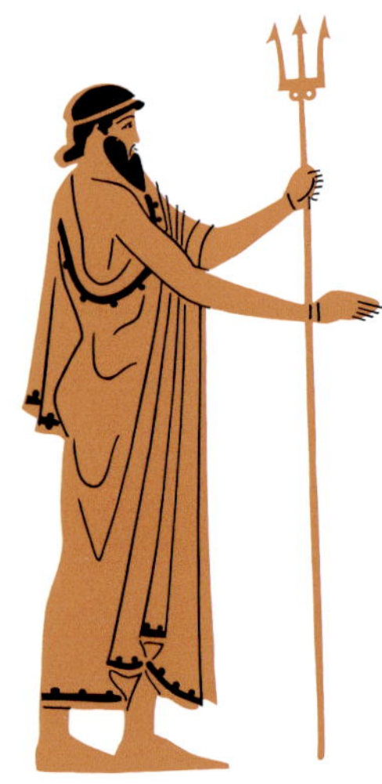

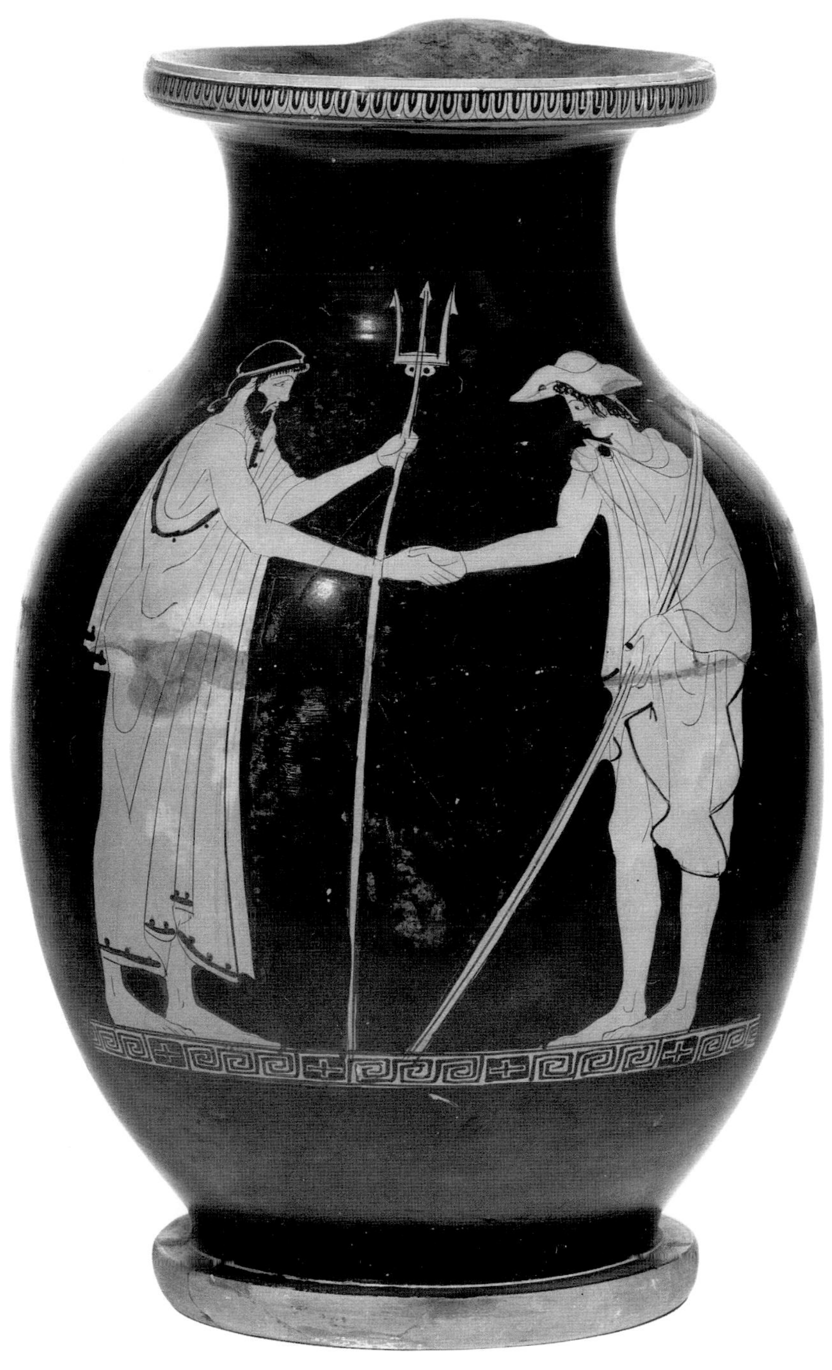

YALE OINOCHOE

Scenes from daily life became increasingly common in Athenian vase painting during the course of the fifth century B.C. Pictures of women at home were especially popular, showing them engaged in characteristic tasks such as spinning or working at wool, washing, dressing, or primping, or sitting quietly, alone or with other women, holding a mirror or a cosmetic vessel or playing a musical instrument. Here a woman holds a bundle of clothing which she is about to put into an open chest. She wears a *chiton* (a lightweight pleated linen garment with full billowing sleeves) and over it a *himation*, which wraps around her body and over one shoulder. Her hair is tied back with a hairnet covering the lower portion, a hairstyle usually worn by unmarried women, and she wears a simple band (a fillet) around her head. The chair behind the figure and the mirror (left) and fillet or wreath hanging on the wall are further indications of a domestic interior.

Much of our information about ancient Greek furniture comes from scenes like this one. The chest has a hinged lid with a lip that overlaps the front edge, and its feet are in the form of lion's paws, a feature familiar to us from American and English furniture. The chest appears to be made of wood, and a star-rosette (either painted or carved) decorates its side. The chair is a popular and purely Greek type. Judging from representations of it in use, it is a comfortable chair, with a rounded back and often (as here) a seat cushion. It seems to have had a woven seat. The back supports and the back legs were carved as single continuous pieces, and the legs were joined to the seat with dowels or mortise and tenon. In terms both of elegance of line and of proportion, this type of chair is the most eloquent expression in furniture of the Greek sense of harmony and grace.

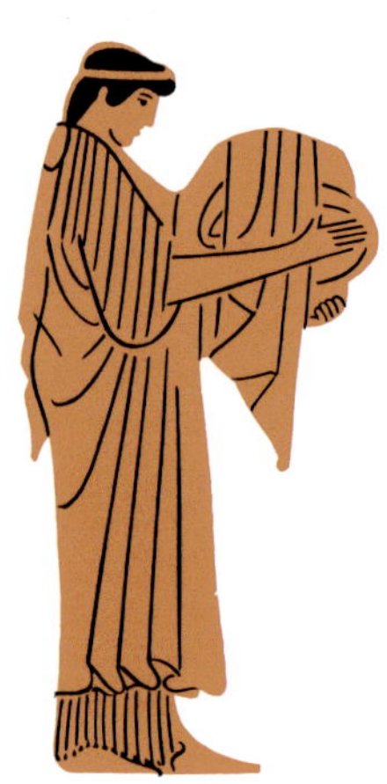

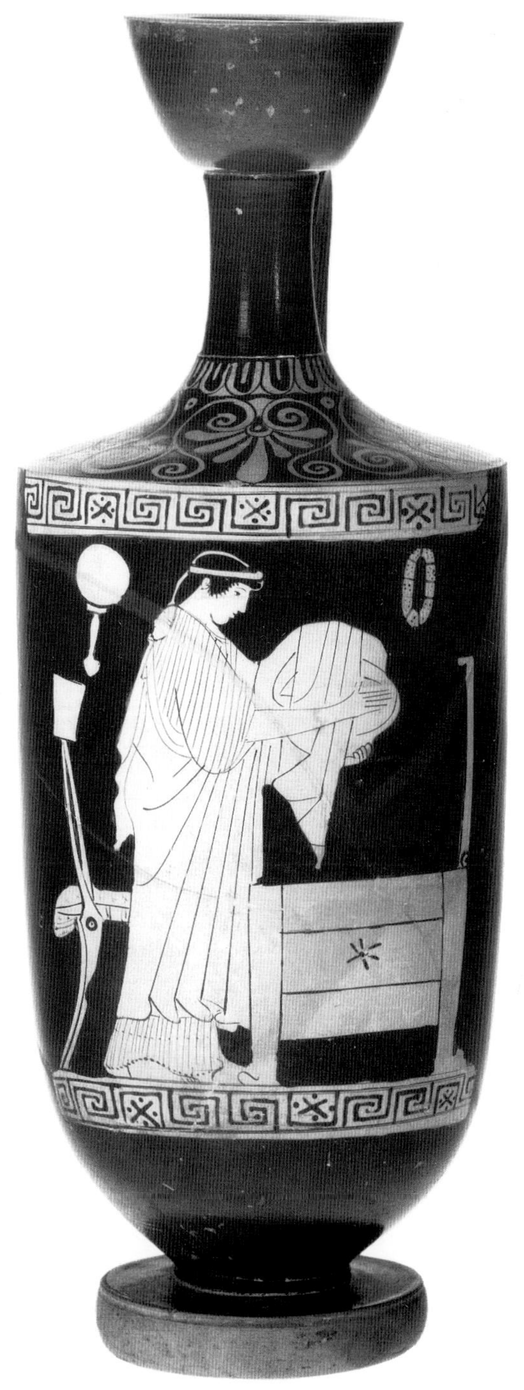

LEKYTHOS WITH DOMESTIC SCENE

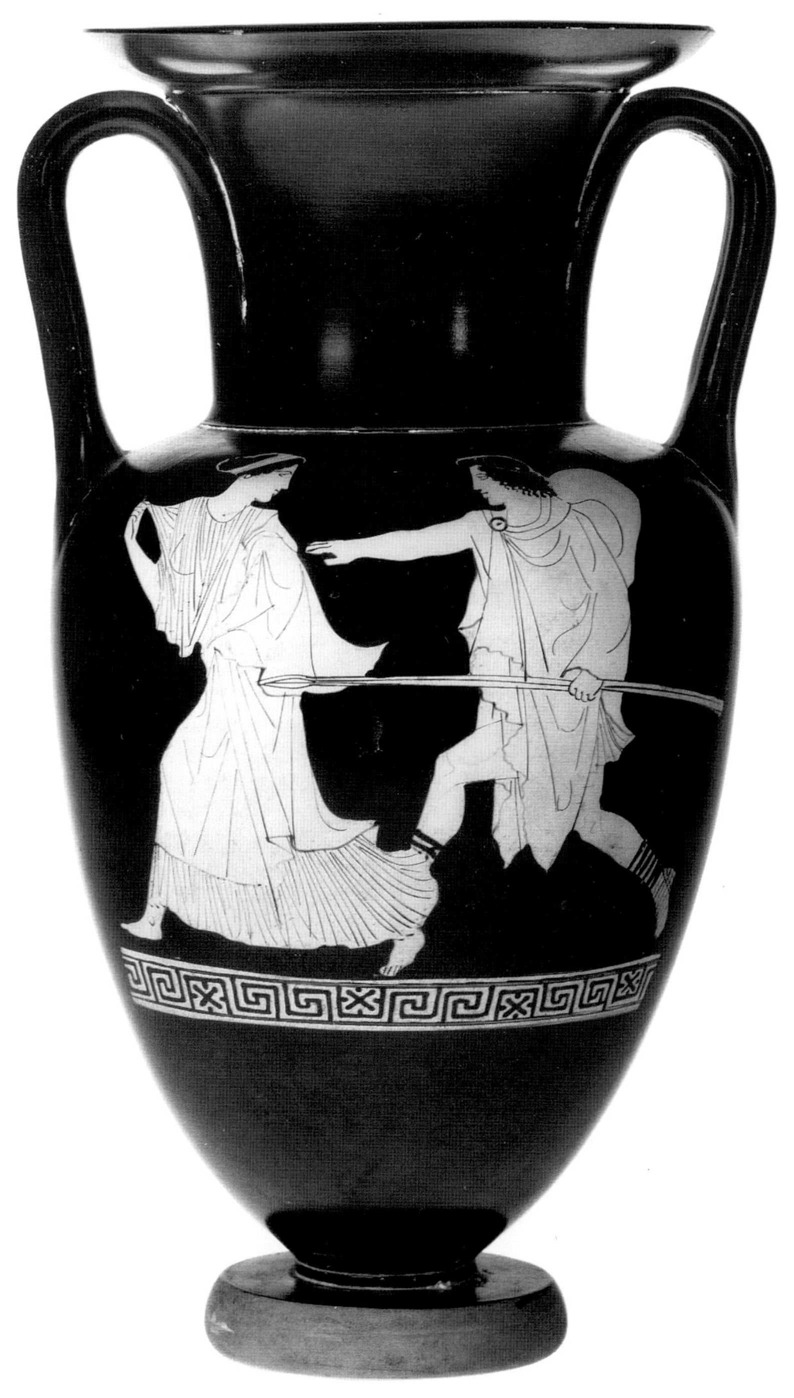

AMPHORA WITH PURSUIT SCENE

32

Athenian vase painting in the time of Perikles was strongly influenced by the sculptures Pheidias designed for the Parthenon (447-432 B.C.), the major new public building of its day. First the stately, Olympian figures of the procession on the Parthenon frieze inspired the style of Classical vase painters like the Achilles Painter, and later the more complex drapery systems of the pedimental sculptures appear in vases by the Eretria Painter and others.

The Phiale Painter, considered a pupil of the Achilles Painter, manifests the Pheidian spirit as well. Like the Painter of Munich 2335 (see p. 34), the Phiale Painter produced white-ground funerary lekythoi, and it is in these vases that his style is closest to that of his teacher. The Phiale Painter's red-figure work, of which this amphora is typical, often has scenes with more action than the funerary vases, but even pursuit scenes such as this one show some of the restraint of the Pheidian style when compared with their Late Archaic and Early Classical predecessors.

The painter has not identified the young man or the woman he pursues. The man wears a travelling costume similar to that often worn by Theseus (see pp. 28-29), but without an inscription naming him we cannot be sure of his identity.

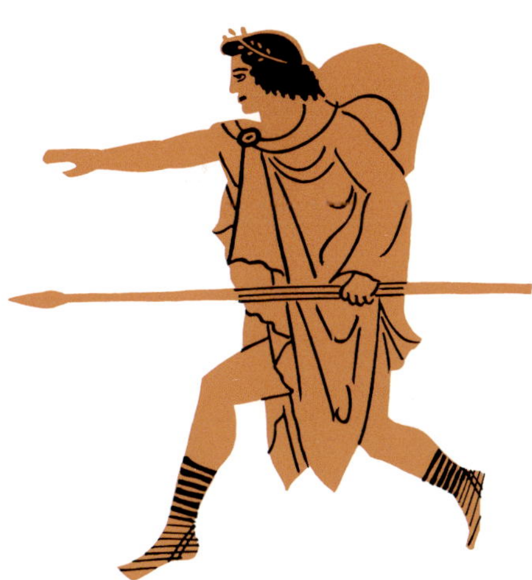

Offerings at the tombs of the Athenian dead often included pots filled with oil, and in the Classical period (ca. 450-430 B.C.) lekythoi decorated in a special technique known as white-ground became the favored choice for this purpose. The white slip that covered the cylindrical body of the vase was less stable than the black glaze of black- and red-figure vases, and the tendency of this slip to wear off made white-ground lekythoi more suitable for one-time funerary offerings than for everyday use. The white slip provided a neutral background for the extensive use of colored washes that characterizes these lekythoi. Here, for example, red is used for the man's cloak and the woman's dress, the latter mostly lost, and yellow for his hat and the bronze phiale (offering dish) that she holds. The drawing style is free and fluent, and in vases of around 440-430 B.C., like this one, strongly influenced by the sculptural style of the Parthenon frieze.

The subjects represented on white-ground lekythoi generally reflect their funerary associations. Scenes of offerings at the tomb, of which this one is typical, are common, and they contribute to our understanding of Athenian funerary customs. As is the case with stone grave monuments of the fourth century B.C., however, it remains unclear, perhaps deliberately, whether the deceased is represented in these scenes. The separation of the two figures by the grave monument may suggest the separation between this world and the next. The woman, who brings the offerings to the tomb, must still be living, leaving the man, in the normal Greek travelling costume of a short cloak, sandals, and a broad brimmed hat, as a figure that could represent the deceased on his final journey to the Underworld. The quiet poignancy of these figures reflects the Classical Greek ideal of dignity and restraint in the face of death or sorrow.

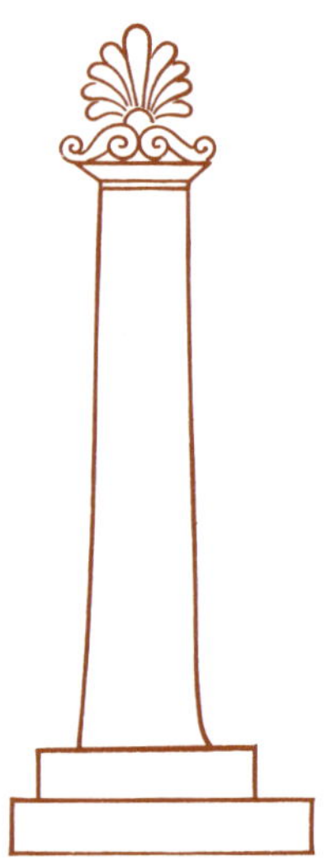

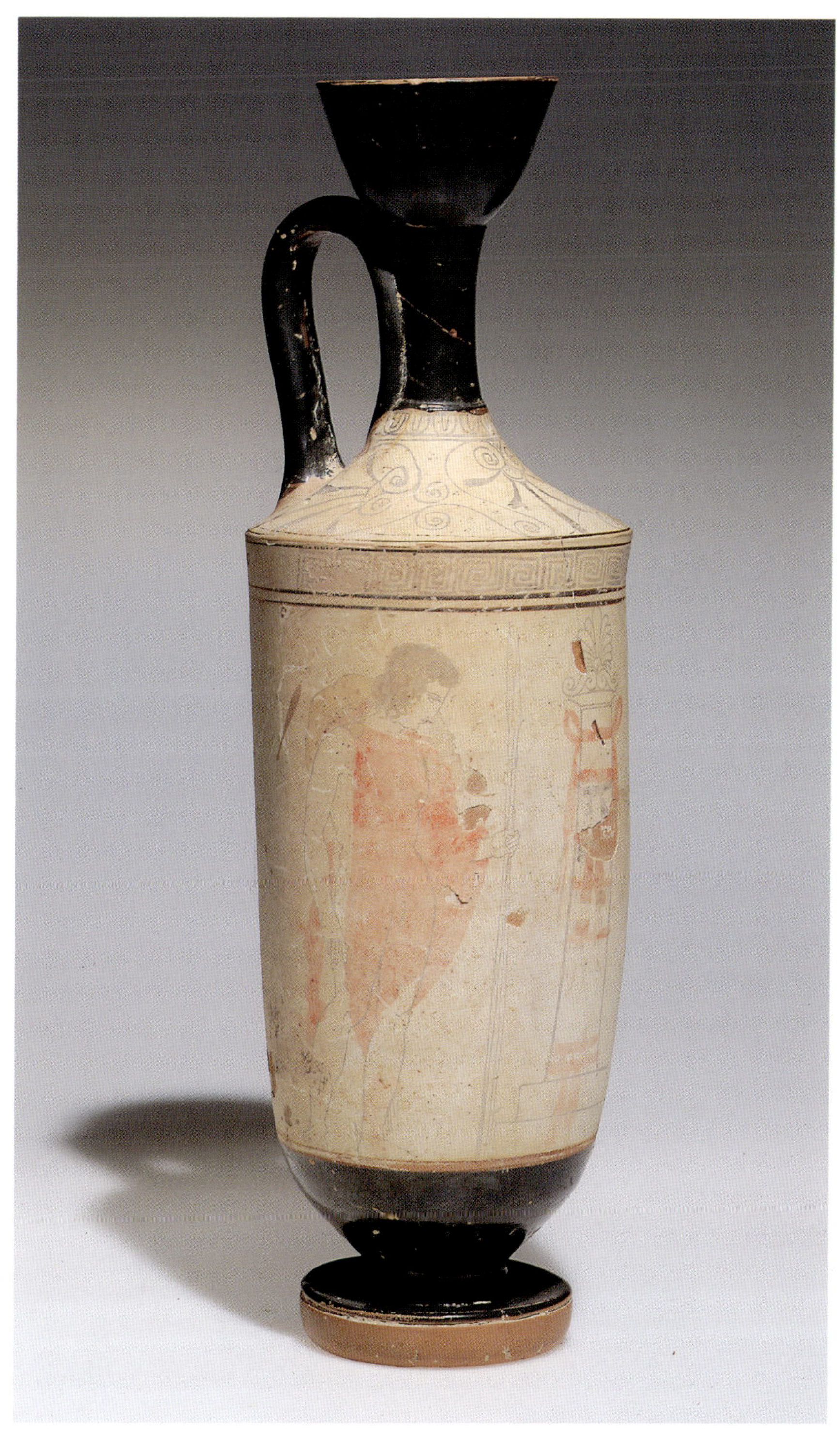

WHITE-GROUND

FUNERARY

LEKYTHOS

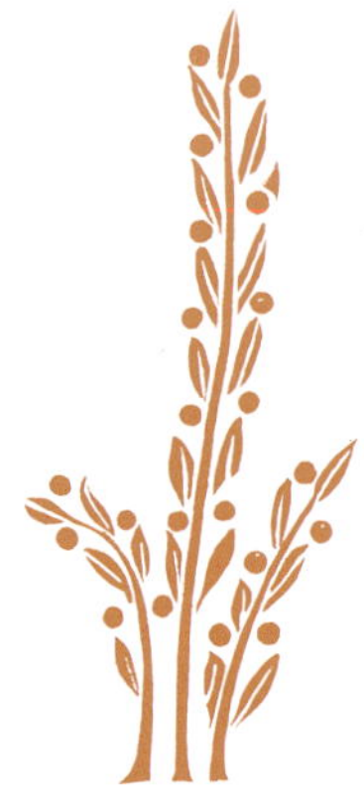

During the last quarter of the fifth century B.C., when Athens was engaged in the disastrous Peloponnesian War (431-404 B.C.), a new stylistic trend emerged in vase painting. Vases by the Meidias Painter, the outstanding practitioner of the style, and his followers show a fascination with complex patterns of swirling drapery that are characteristic of the graceful and elegant females in late fifth-century Athenian sculpture. In the hands of the vase painters, the style became a pretty and rather decorative one, and when complemented by subjects frequently related to women, beauty, and love, it created an elegant fantasy world in which Aphrodite and Eros were the patron deities.

The style and subject matter were particularly well suited to small vases like this squat lekythos which were used by women as perfume containers. Aphrodite appears here as in so many Meidian vases, but the real subject of this scene is Poseidon, as a lover. The sea god is recognizable by his trident, and he stands facing his wife Amphitrite (only partially preserved), who sits in the center of the composition. Next to Amphitrite is a hydria (water jar), and on her lap she holds the cushion that would have rested under the hydria as she carried it on her head. Poseidon is accompanied by Amymone (right), whom he seduced, and Aphrodite is seated to the left, perhaps as a symbol of desire, like the hare, which was a common gift between lovers. How different is this rather effeminate Poseidon from the majestic seated figure receiving Nike's offering on the krater by the Aegisthus Painter (see p. 26).

Plants, apparently laurel bushes, have been added to the picture to suggest a landscape setting. The impression of a rocky landscape is enhanced by the uneven ground levels on which the figures rest: Amymone stands on a lower level than Poseidon; Amphitrite and Aphrodite are seated on an even higher level. The use of landscape in vase painting derives from famous wall paintings in Athens, now lost, but known to us from descriptions in ancient literature.

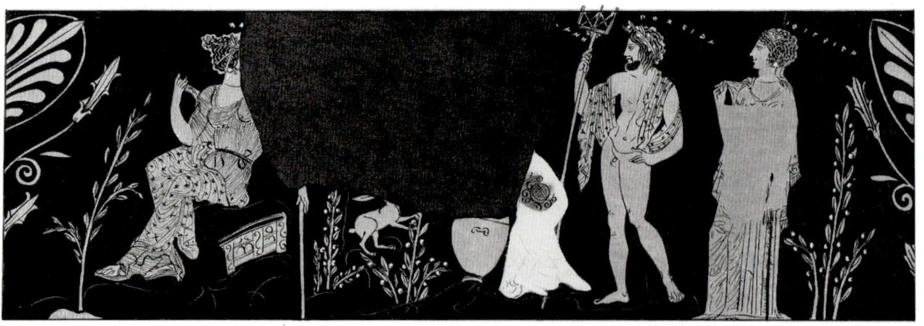

ROLLED-OUT DRAWING SHOWING POSEIDON AS LOVER

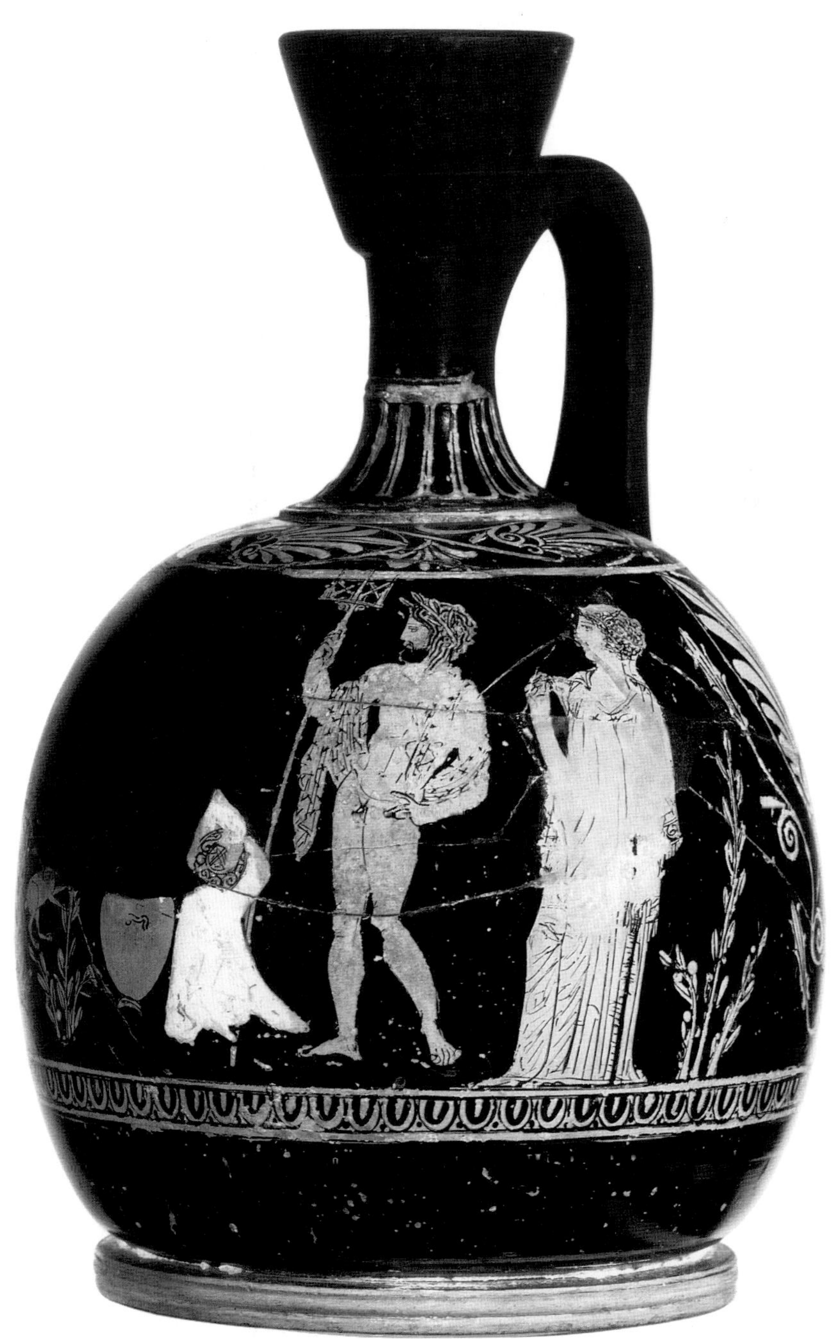

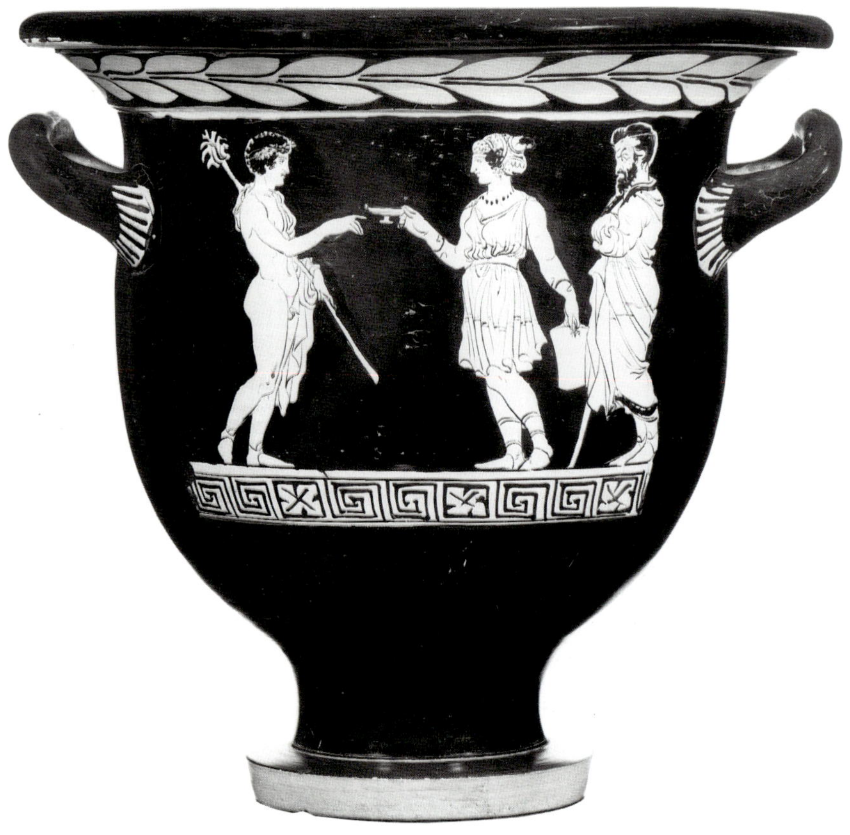

Red-figure Bell Krater by the Dolon Painter

The lucrative export trade that had brought Athenian vases to Greek colonies in Italy and Sicily for more than a century broke down during the Peloponnesian War, and so Athenian potters, already resident in these colonies, began to make their own pottery to fill the gap. The earliest of these so-called South Italian vases were very close to their Athenian models. This krater by the Dolon Painter, for example, clearly recalls Athenian compositions, poses, and drapery style, and shows equal similarity in its shape and ornament. Later South Italian vase painting developed along its own lines into a more ornate, florid style unparalleled elsewhere.

The Dolon Painter's krater depicts Dionysos, left, conversing with a maenad, who offers him a cup of wine, and a silen, recognizable by his goat ears. The silen has been given a rather comic treatment in comparison to the other two figures, with his ears, his bulging eyes, and his arched eyebrows creating something like a comic mask. Theatrical subjects, like Greek drama itself, were popular in Italy, and comic theatre, including some peculiarly local variations, inspired numerous South Italian vases.

38

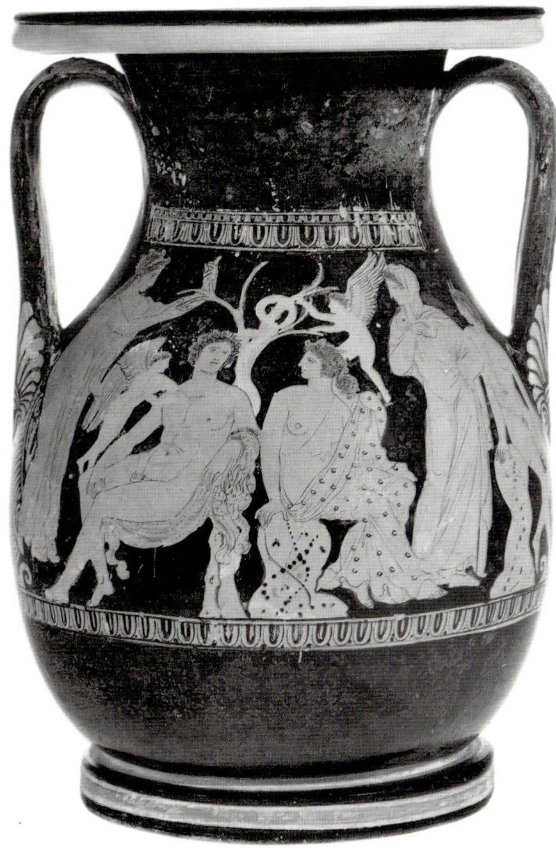

Red-figure Pelike in the Early Kerch Style

In the fourth century B.C., as Athens began to recover from the effects of the Peloponnesian War, Athenian potters found a new market for their red-figure vases in the cities along the coast of the Black Sea. A large group of these vases found in the South Russian city of Kerch have given the city's name to the last phase of Attic red-figure vase painting. The Kerch style carries on from the ornate late fifth-century style of the Meidias Painter and his school (see p. 36), but Kerch style figures are both more stately and more sculptural. At their best, they have a refined statuesque quality that recalls the sculpture of Praxiteles.

Herakles in the Garden of the Hesperides, shown on this early Kerch style pelike, remained, unlike the other labors of Herakles, a popular subject for Greek vase painters well into the fourth century B.C. The nature of the labor, in which Herakles goes to the garden to retrieve the apples of immortality, made it easily adaptable to the format of the quiet garden or interior domestic scenes favored by fourth-century painters. Herakles, young and elegant in spite of the rigors of his previous eleven labors, is

39

posed in the garden like a seated statue, relaxed, and surrounded by the lovely Hesperides, who have assumed equally statuesque poses. The garden is quiet, and even the guardian serpent in the tree appears benign.

Athenian and South Italian red-figure vase painting died out after the last quarter of the fourth century. The nature of the technique prevented its practitioners from adopting the stylistic innovations, particularly the use of shading and a broad range of subtly varied colors, that characterized monumental painting at this time. Although some adaptations of these techniques were made for funerary vessels (e.g., the Canosa ware of South Italy), the role of painted vases was increasingly filled by molded pottery and vessels of precious metals and glass.

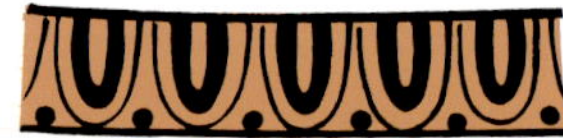

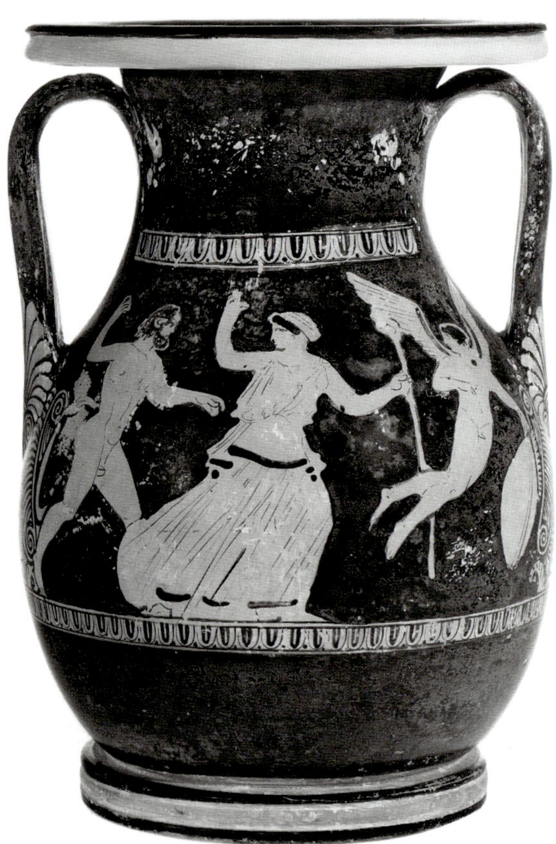

SUGGESTED READING

P. E. Arias, M. Hirmer, and B. Shefton, *Greek Vase Painting* (New York, 1961).

J. D. Beazley, *The Development of Attic Black-figure*, 2nd ed., rev. (Berkeley and Los Angeles, 1986).

J. D. Beazley, *Attic White Lekythoi* (London, 1938).

J. Boardman, *Athenian Black-figure Vases* (New York, 1974).

J. Boardman, *Athenian Red-figure Vases: The Archaic Period* (London, 1975).

R. M. Cook, *Greek Painted Pottery* (London, 1972).

J. Henle, *Greek Myths: A Vase Painter's Notebook* (Bloomington, Indiana, 1973).

M. G. Kanowski, *Containers of Classical Greece* (St. Lucia, Queensland, Australia, 1984).

J. V. Noble, *The Techniques of Painted Attic Pottery* (London, 1966).

G. M. A. Richter, *Attic Red-figure Vases: A Survey* (New Haven, 1958).

NOTES ON ILLUSTRATIONS

p. 6 *Mycenaean Vases: Stirrup Jar,* ca. 1200-1100 B.C., H. 11 cm. (4¼ in.), Stoddard Collection, 1913.34; *Piriform Jar,* ca. 1400-1300 B.C., H. 14.3 cm. (5⅝ in.), Yale University Art Gallery, 1967.74.2; *Bridge-spouted Bowl,* ca. 1300-1200 B.C., H. 15.6 cm. (6⅛ in.), Stoddard Collection, 1913.44

p. 8 *Protogeometric Amphora,* ca. 1050-1000 B.C., H. 39.7 cm. (15⅝ in.), Stoddard Collection, 1913.50

p. 9 *Late Geometric Vases: Pomegranate Vase from the Dipylon Workshop,* ca. 750-725 B.C., H. 10.2 cm. (4 in.), Stoddard Collection, 1913.60; *Olpe,* ca. 740-700 B.C., H. 17.6 cm. (7 in.), Stoddard Collection, 1913.55; *Fragment of a Krater by the Kunze Painter, from the Dipylon Workshop,* ca. 750-725 B.C., H. 10 cm. (4 in.; joins Louvre A519), Classics Department Transfer, 1981.61.271

p. 10 *Corinthian Griffin-bird Alabastron,* ca. 625-600 B.C., H. 10.5 cm. (4 in.), The Rebecca Darlington Stoddard Fund, 1977.83

p. 11 *Komast Cup by the KY Painter,* showing padded dancers, ca. 580-570 B.C., H. 8.7 cm. (3⅜ in.), D. 19.3 cm. (7½ in.), Stoddard Collection, 1913.102

p. 13 *Black-figure Amphora attributed to Group E,* showing the birth of Athena (side 1) and a frontal four-horse chariot (side 2), ca. 560-540 B.C., H. 40.9 cm (16 in.), Leonard C. Hanna, Jr., B.A. 1913, Fund, 1983.22

p. 14 *Red-figure Plate by Paseas,* showing the rape of Kassandra, ca. 520-510 B.C., D. 18.7 cm. (7⅜ in.), Stoddard Collection, 1913.169

p. 17 *Red-figure Kylix near the Gales Painter,* showing a drinking party (*symposion*) scene, ca. 510-500 B.C., H. 9.2 cm. (3⅝ in.), D. 22.3 cm. (8¾ in.), Stoddard Collection, 1913.163; *Red-figure Kylix near the Chaire Painter,* showing a jumper, ca. 500 B.C., D. 17.8 cm. (7 in.), Stoddard Collection, 1913.162

p. 18 *Black-figure Lekythos by the Edinburgh Painter,* showing Apollo driving a chariot pulled by lions and boars, ca. 500 B.C., H. 32.1 cm. (12⅝ in.), Stoddard Collection, 1913.111

p. 20 *Panathenaic Prize Amphora by the Kleophrades Painter,* showing Athena (side 1) and a four-horse chariot (side 2), ca. 490 B.C., H. 65.5 cm. (25¾ in.), Gift of Frederic W. Stephens, B.A. 1858, 1909.13

p. 22 *Red-figure Amphora by the Berlin Painter,* showing Athena (side 1) and Hermes (side 2), ca. 480 B.C., H. 32.7 cm. (12⅞ in.), Stoddard Collection, 1913.133

SHAPES OF GREEK VASES

Alabastron: perfume container, often used by women, with a long drop- or pear-shaped body and a narrow neck.

Amphora: storage jar with two vertical loop handles, from neck to body; of two basic types: 1) neck-amphora, with separately articulated neck meeting the body at an angle and 2) one-piece amphora, with neck merging into the body in one continuous curve.

Aryballos: small oil container, often used by athletes. There are rounded, pointed, and piriform types.

Hydria: water jar with three handles: two at the sides for lifting and carrying and a third at the back for pouring; carried on the head, on a cushion.

Kantharos: drinking cup with a goblet-shaped bowl, high vertical loop handles, and a stemmed foot (also a stemless variety).

Kylix: drinking cup with a wide, shallow bowl, two curved, nearly horizontal handles, and a stemmed foot (also a stemless variety).

Krater: large bowl with a wide mouth, two handles, and generally a foot, used for mixing wine and water. Variants based on differences of profile and position of handles: *calyx krater, column krater, bell krater.*

Lekythos: oil container, used by men, women, and as funerary offerings, with a cylindrical body, tall neck, deep mouth, single handle at the back. *Squat lekythos:* variant with squat globular body, broad base, and no distinct shoulder.

Oinochoe: pitcher or jug, with single handle, widely varied in shape. *Olpe:* variant with bulbous body and rounded mouth, the neck and body merging in a continuous curve; *chous:* later development of the olpe, with a trefoil mouth.

Pelike: storage jar with two handles, shaped like a one-piece amphora but with a sagging pear-shaped body.

Pyxis: small box-like container with lid, usually cylindrical or with concave sides, used by women for cosmetics and jewelry.

Skyphos: drinking cup with a deep body, two horizontal handles, and a low foot. *Glaux:* variant with one vertical and one horizontal handle.

Stamnos: storage jar with wide mouth, wide upper body tapering to a low foot, and two nearly horizontal handles.

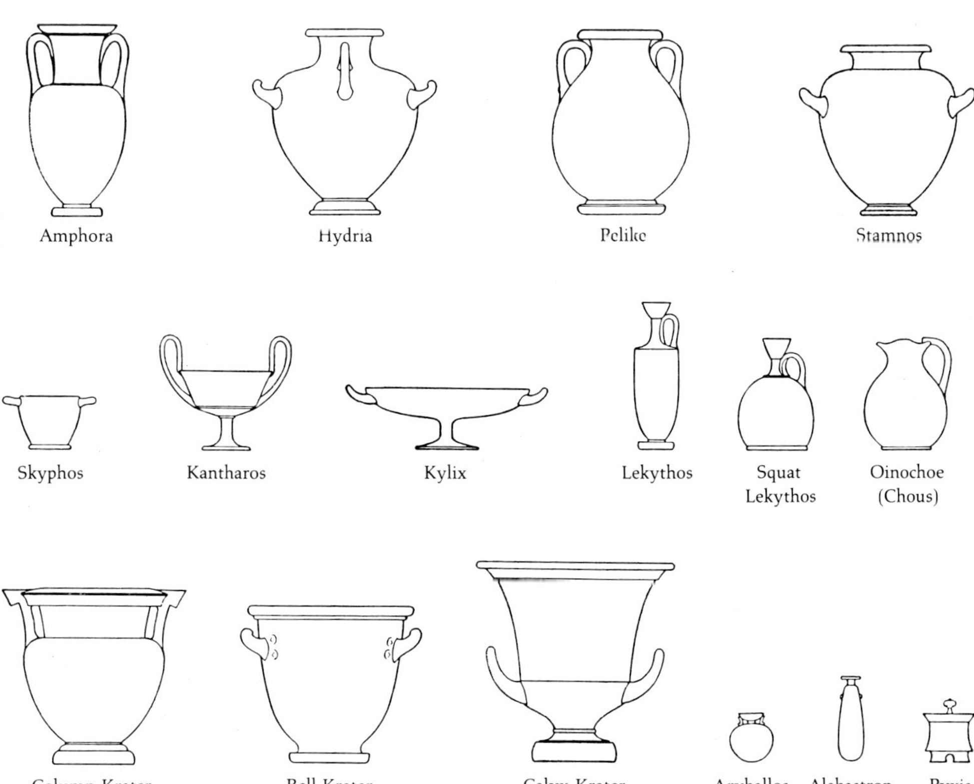

After G. M. A. Richter, *A Handbook of Greek Art* (London, 1965)

Design and line drawings by Sue Allen.

Photography by Joseph Szaszfai.

Photograph on page 27 courtesy of McAlpine Ancient Art, London.

Typesetting by Brevis Press and Meriden-Stinehour.

Printing and binding by Dai Nippon Printing Company, Ltd.